Elite • 255

The 'Grossdeutschland' Division in World War II

The German Army's premier combat unit

JAMES F. SLAUGHTER

ILLUSTRATED BY RAMIRO BUJEIRO
Series editors Martin Windrow & Nick Reynolds

OSPREY PUBLISHING
Bloomsbury Publishing Plc
Kemp House, Chawley Park, Cumnor Hill, Oxford OX2 9PH, UK
29 Earlsfort Terrace, Dublin 2, Ireland
1385 Broadway, 5th Floor, New York, NY 10018, USA
E-mail: info@ospreypublishing.com
www.ospreypublishing.com

OSPREY is a trademark of Osprey Publishing Ltd

First published in Great Britain in 2024

A catalogue record for this book is available from the British Library.

ISBN: PB 9781472855923; eBook 9781472855930;
ePDF 9781472855947; XML 9781472855954

24 25 26 27 28   10 9 8 7 6 5 4 3 2 1

Index by Rob Munro
Typeset by PDQ Digital Media Solutions, Bungay, UK
Printed and bound in India by Replika Press Private Ltd.

Osprey Publishing supports the Woodland Trust, the UK's leading woodland
conservation charity.

To find out more about our authors and books visit
www.ospreypublishing.com. Here you will find extracts, author
interviews, details of forthcoming events and the option to sign up for our
newsletter.

Artist's note

Readers may care to note that the original paintings from which the colour
plates in this book were prepared are available for private sale. All
reproduction copyright whatsoever is retained by the publishers. All
enquiries should be addressed to:

ramirobujeiro@gmail.com

The publishers regret that they can enter into no correspondence upon
this matter.

Front cover, above: SdKfz 250 half-tracked personnel carriers cross the
Russian steppe. (Nik Cornish at www.stavka.org.uk)

Title-page illustration: Photographed in November 1943, this GD soldier
has an anti-tank grenade fitted to his Kar 98k rifle. (ullstein bild/ullstein bild
via Getty Images)

CONTENTS

THE 'GROSSDEUTSCHLAND' DIVISION IN WORLD WAR II

THE GERMAN ARMY'S PREMIER COMBAT UNIT

ORIGINS

The origins of Panzergrenadier-Division 'Großdeutschland' (GD) are to be found in the Wachregiment Berlin, established in early 1921 but quickly disbanded. While Wachregiment Berlin's primary functions were parades and ceremonial guards, it maintained the ability, and some would argue projected the threat to practise violence on behalf of the state. Soon thereafter, the Kommando der Wachtruppe was established, and in this organization, the nature of the future GD can be discerned. The *Kommando* was staffed by soldiers from all over Germany, usually for a period of three months, and clearly had a mostly ceremonial intent; *Großdeutschland* ('greater Germany') thus provided the nexus for the future division. The unit was an enjoyable temporary post for many soldiers. German units were regional, and usually quite local, and the camaraderie provided by soldiers from other areas who often had different accents, food, outlooks and regional quirks and philosophies was welcomed.

Beginning in 1934, the Nazis fundamentally transformed Germany. The Wehrmacht began to rearm rapidly. In 1934, the Kommando der Wachtruppe was redesignated Wachtruppe Berlin, and in June 1937 as Wachregiment Berlin. The unit was still largely ceremonial in nature and paraded not only for the public, but for a variety of dignitaries and diplomats whom the Nazi elite were eager to impress or intimidate through overt demonstrations

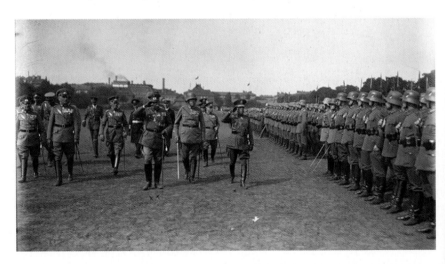

Amid a group of senior officers, Generalleutnant Wilhelm Heye of the Reichswehr and Argentine General Severo Toranzo salute the Kommando der Wachtruppe, August 1929. (Bundesarchiv, Bild 102-08315/ CC-BY-SA 3.0 de)

A *Schütze* wears the regiment's new dress uniform, 16 June 1939. GD's eventual divisional symbol, the *Stahlhelm*, equipped the soldiers throughout the war. The Stahlhelm 35 that most troops wore in 1940 was an evolution of the Stahlhelm 16 first issued during World War I. As with the Stahlhelm 16, the Stahlhelm 35 was a solid piece of engineering. Utilizing an innovative stamping process that kept the thickness of the manganese steel almost completely uniform, the Stahlhelm 35's centre of gravity was located at the crown above the centre of the head, which resulted in remarkable stability; even without the chinstrap, the helmet resisted coming off. Moreover, the flaring shield around the neck not only helped keep water at bay, but also gave meaningful protection to the neck. Vents on the helmet helped to dissipate pressure from nearby explosions and thus reduce the possibility of injury to the soldier. (Süddeutsche Zeitung Photo/Alamy Stock Photo)

On 2 August 1939, a *Grosser Zapfenstreich* ('Grand Tattoo') was held at the Kleiner Tiergarten, Moabit, Berlin, to mark the 25th anniversary of the German mobilization for World War I. Note the use of the standard Heer parade uniforms and the absence of *Ärmelstreifen*. Oberstleutnant Wilhelm-Hunold von Stockhausen, the regimental commander, and Major Werner Frotscher, the commander of the 5. Kompanie, are moving towards the camera. Stockhausen led IR (mot.) GD from its formation, missing part of the French campaign through illness but leading his regiment in the Balkans and the early stages of Operation *Barbarossa*. Promoted to *Generalmajor* in April 1941, Stockhausen was succeeded by Oberst Walter Hörnlein on 1 August 1941 and subsequently commanded the 1. Schützen-Brigade and then the 281. Sicherungs-Division. (Süddeutsche Zeitung Photo/Alamy Stock Photo)

of strength. In June 1939, the order came for the Wachregiment Berlin to convert to Infanterie-Regiment 'Großdeutschland'.

THE WAR BEGINS

On 1 September 1939, Germany invaded Poland. Despite Berlin's proximity to Poland, Infanterie-Regiment (mot.) 'Großdeutschland' (IR (mot.) GD) did not participate in operations. The regiment was still in the process of formal organization and establishment as a regular combat unit, and although the pace of training increased, the relatively short duration of combat operations in Poland precluded the need to commit the regiment.

Like most Heer (Army) units, IRGD underwent extensive training during the winter of 1939/40 in western Germany. The training during the period was quite intense and the winter weather made conditions more difficult for the regiment's troops. The time was well spent, however, and it allowed IR (mot.) GD to integrate its attached support troops and work them into operations. In addition, IR (mot.) GD's four battalions were able to train together, sometimes with live ammunition, and in concert with other units. By the end of March 1940, the regiment was cohesive, very well established and thoroughly trained in its battle drills.

With Oberstleutnant Wilhelm-Hunold von Stockhausen absent through illness, Oberstleutnant Gerhard Graf von Schwerin commanded IR (mot.) GD and its attached units during *Fall Gelb* (Spaeter 1992: 56–57). During the invasion of France, the regiment was provided with considerable assets for a unit of its size. For *Fall Gelb*, the regiment consisted of four battalions of four

OPPOSITE
The new dress uniforms decreed for IR (mot.) GD are modelled by (left) a *Schütze* wearing a *Mantel* and gloves and (right) a *Hauptfeldwebel* with the *Deutsches Sportabzeichen* and the standard NCO's sabre, 16 June 1939. (Süddeutsche Zeitung Photo/Alamy Stock Photo

companies each. The first three battalions (I.–III.) were rifle battalions, each with three rifle companies (each with 12 light machine guns and three 5cm mortars) and one machine-gun company (12 medium machine guns and six 8cm mortars). The IV. (heavy) Bataillon, led by Schneider, was composed of: a light-infantry-gun company, numbered 13 (commanded by von Massow), equipped with six 7.5cm leInfG; an anti-tank company (14; Beck-Broichsitter) armed with 12 3.7cm PaK; a heavy-infantry-gun company (15; März) with four 15cm sInfG; and an assault-gun company (16, formerly Sturmgeschütz-Batterie 640; von Egloffstein) with six 7.5cm Sturmgeschütz III assault guns. In addition, IRGD had a supply column (Versorgungstruppen 400) attached, as well as Sturm-Pionier-Bataillon 43, with three *Pionier* companies and a bridging detachment.

FALL GELB AND AFTER

On 10 May 1940, two companies of Oberstleutnant Eugen Garski's III./ IR (mot.) GD were engaged in Operation *NiWi* in southern Belgium, in which troops delivered by air in Fieseler Fi 156 Storch aircraft – each capable of carrying only two soldiers – were to take and hold vital points on the intended lines of advance. One contingent, 11./IR (mot.) GD under Hauptmann Walther Krüger, was tasked with seizing ground near Nives, while 10./IR (mot.) GD, under Garski's direct command, was to be landed near Witry. In the event, while Garski's aircraft landed in the correct place at 0600hrs, he found that he could muster only nine men in all. Much of Garski's contingent got lost and landed elsewhere, nearer Nives than Witry; Krüger's company was also dispersed. While Garski managed to evade capture on the Witry–Neufchâteau road, reinforcements under Leutnant Obermeier decided to block the Neufchâteau–Bastogne road and held their position throughout the day. Meanwhile, Krüger was able to regroup and capture Witry at 1400hrs, making contact with lead elements of Generalleutnant Friedrich Kirchner's 1. Panzer-Division soon afterwards; it subsequently became clear that Garski's men had cut the communications links to a small party of Belgian troops at Bodange, meaning the Belgians never received an order to withdraw if attacked and opened fire upon the motorcycle troops leading Kirchner's advance, thereby stalling the German effort by a full day. The Nives contingent established contact with the 2. Panzer-Division on the morning of 11 May.

The rest of IR (mot.) GD crossed the Belgian border on the morning of 10 May 1940, and received its baptism of fire at Etalle, at the hands of French cavalry and motorized reconnaissance troops who subsequently withdrew. Major Hans-Hermann Föst was killed on 10 May: Major Alfred Greim took his place as commander of II./IR (mot.) GD. Oberstleutnant Otto Köhler, commander of I./IR (mot.) GD, was detached to take command of Infanterie-Regiment 69, and was replaced by Hauptmann Föllmer.

On 11 May, I./IR (mot.) GD attacked French forces in the village of Suxy, applying the combined-arms tactics learned in training. On the evening of 12 May, the regiment was redeployed to the XIX. Armeekorps, crossing into France in the early morning of 13 May. The bulk of ID (mot.) GD's assaulting troops had virtually no rest, but the tempo of operations had to be maintained to keep the Allied forces on the back foot throughout the campaign.

Generalmajor Gerhard Graf von Schwerin, 1943. As an *Oberstleutnant*, Schwerin led I./IR (mot.) GD from October 1939 and became the regiment's deputy commander in February 1940. He assumed command of IR (mot.) GD during 10–18 May 1940, as the regimental commander was ill. Transferred to North Africa in early 1941, Schwerin subsequently fought in the Soviet Union, Western Europe and Italy, and ended the war as a *General der Panzertruppe* commanding the LXXVI. Panzerkorps. (ullstein bild/ullstein bild via Getty Images)

Following a tiring approach march in warm conditions, IR (mot.) GD and its attached units forced an assault crossing of the Meuse River close to Sedan under extremely heavy fire during the late afternoon of 13 May. Tasked with crossing the river and seizing Hill 247 behind it, II. and III./IR (mot.) GD used an assortment of rubber rafts during the assault, conducted alongside elements of Sturm-Pionier-Bataillon 43 in the teeth of brutal French fire. Although many of the French units in the area at the time were not first-line units, they fought extremely fiercely, and it took repeated Luftwaffe bombardments and point-blank fire from German artillery to ensure that the crossing was successful (Doughty 1990: 147). Once across, GD troops engaged in house-to-house fighting and stormed several bunkers, seizing Hill 247 by early evening. The regiment's vehicles and heavy weapons were ferried across and the anti-tank guns of Oberleutnant Helmut Beck-Broichsitter's 14./IR (mot.) GD prepared for the inevitable French counter-attack; during the morning of 14 May, Beck-Broichsitter's men knocked out French tanks and armoured cars near Chémery. Shortly after German troops captured Chémery, German dive-bombers mistakenly attacked the GD forces; among the dead was Oberstleutnant Siegfried Mahler, commander of Sturm-Pionier-Bataillon 43.

The worst fighting of the campaign was yet to come for GD, however. Following the crossing of the Meuse, the French threw considerable forces into the fight at the town of Stonne to try to re-establish control of the area and prevent the regiment and the other German units from exploiting the breach. During 15–17 May, the regiment and its attached units fought a brutal battle in Stonne and on the surrounding heights against heavy French resistance, including determined French tank assaults, and heavy artillery bombardments. Stonne would change hands 17 times in three days before the Germans finally prevailed. Again, Sturm-Pionier-Bataillon 43 assisted with the house-to-house assaults that were their particular speciality. Beck-Broichsitter's anti-tank gunners also came to understand how underpowered their 3.7cm PaK guns were, especially against the frontal armour of the newest generation of Allied tanks. At this point, the regiment had suffered 103 killed, 442 wounded and 25 missing (Spaeter 1992: 97).

Having recovered from illness, Oberstleutnant von Stockhausen returned to command IR (mot.) GD on 18 May. Following a brief rest period to consolidate, resupply and recuperate, the regiment moved towards the English Channel to participate in the fighting in the vicinity of Dunkirk.

The third pattern of officer's *Ärmelstreifen* (cuff title), worn on the right sleeve from October 1940 onwards. There were four distinct styles of GD cuff title worn during 1939–45. The first was silver *Fraktur* on green, while the second added 'Inf.-Regt.' before 'Großdeutschland'. The third type, the type most associated with the GD units, bore *Sütterlin* script in silver on black and is by far the most common surviving example. The fourth type, issued very late in the war, featured copperplate lettering in silver on black (Pritchett 2010: 2.19). Officers usually purchased officer's-quality *Ärmelstreifen* that frequently featured silver bullion letters and these would remain widely worn, remarkably, even during the latter stages of the war. (INTERFOTO/Alamy Stock Photo)

The third pattern of enlisted man's *Ärmelstreifen*, used from October 1940 onwards. GD's distinctive insignia set it apart from the rest of the *Heer*. The most prominent and noticeable example of this was the *Ärmelstreifen* members of GD wore on the right sleeve of the *Feldbluse*. While this would at points lead to misidentification as Waffen-SS, the *Ärmelstreifen* began as a way for elite military units to be recognized long before World War II. (INTERFOTO/Alamy Stock Photo)

After being withdrawn on 4 June, the regiment and its attached formations turned south and encountered sporadic, but increasingly formidable French defences. For IR (mot.) GD, the 1940 fighting continued with the attack on the Bois de Berny, a major element of the French Weygand defensive line, on 7 June. Following the capture of the Bois de Berny, the regiment was involved in pursuit operations, and at Erquinvillers was involved in the massacre of African troops in French service who had become prisoners

A

EARLY OPERATIONS

Throughout GD's existence, its uniform, insignia, weapons and personal gear embodied the traditions and practices of the Heer as a whole.

(1) *Schütze*, Wachregiment Berlin, 1938

Standing at attention with his Kar 98k rifle at shoulder arms, this private soldier stares straight ahead. Well-balanced, accurate and reliable, the Kar 98k fired a 7.92×57mm cartridge that was loaded via five-round stripper clips through a guide in the top of the receiver into an internal box magazine.

He wears the early apple-green double-decal Stahlhelm 35 with national tricolour emblem on the right, and the *Waffenrock* (dress tunic) used before the pattern designed specifically for GD use was issued. Most of GD's men wore field equipment almost identical to that worn in World War I. The black leather belt had an aluminium or steel buckle imprinted with the Heer eagle and the traditional motto *Gott mit Uns* ('God is with us'). Most soldiers wore two three-cell Kar 98k magazine pouches dyed black; each pouch carried 30 rounds of 7.92×57mm ammunition for the Kar 98k, although men frequently carried additional ammunition in their pockets. This man's Seitengewehr 84/98 III bayonet with *Troddel* (knot), worn on the left hip, is hidden behind his left leg.

Throughout the first half of World War II, GD's men wore the ubiquitous *Marschstiefel*, a tall leather boot that came up to slightly past mid-calf for most enlisted men and was hobnailed with heel plates. Soldiers wore socks or foot wraps to protect their feet from the boot (breaking-in the boots could be a painful process). Once well dyed and polished, the boots could achieve a relatively good degree of waterproofness, but the hobnails and lack of insulation later proved very problematic in the Soviet Union.

(2) *Hauptmann*, IR (mot.) GD, Yugoslavia, 1941

Map in hand, this *Hauptmann* has had little sleep in the past 36–48 hours. Exhibiting some combat use, his double-decal Stahlhelm 35 has the chinstrap looped over the brim. Officers also wore soft caps trimmed in silver or gold for higher ranks or peaked caps, some of the popular 'crusher' style.

He wears early-style standard 8×30 binoculars around his neck. His officer's-quality M36 tunic has the early GD *Ärmelstreifen* (cuff title), with the usual officer's bullion breast eagle; it is worn with officer's breeches and riding boots. His waist belt supports a map case on the right and a P 08 pistol holster on the left, mounted for cross-draw for a right-handed shooter. The holster flap is slightly loose, suggesting very recent or impending action. In 1939–41 the P 08, aka Luger, was still the predominant semi-automatic pistol in German service. In addition, the P 38 semi-automatic pistol was in serial production; although not widely issued in 1940, it eventually became as ubiquitous as the P 08 and was revered as the 'pistol that never froze in Russia'. Many officers carried private-purchase pistols, however, and a wide variety of personal tastes are reflected in period photographs.

(3) *Unteroffizier*, Signals, IR (mot.) GD, Yugoslavia, 1941

Having discarded his helmet, this signals NCO staring intently at his Torn Fu radio set wears the *Feldmütze* (field cap) and radio headphones. In 1940–42, most of GD's men wore the *Feldmütze* (known as the 'M38') with *Soutache* (piping) in branch-of-service colour; this man has been transferred in from a dedicated signals unit. Although the cap maintained the traditional cockade, the national eagle with the swastika was also present.

His enlisted man's *Feldbluse* (combat jacket) bears NCO *Tresse* (lace) on the collar and *Schulterklappen* (shoulder straps), which are piped for signals. The four-pocket *Feldbluse* had a bottle-green collar and scalloped pockets; there was an internal suspension system that helped the soldier support the weight of the waist belt, and in addition, there was an internal pocket for a wound dressing. A hook-and-loop system held the collar together at the neck, and the collar had buttons to attach a collar liner that not only preserved the garment but also the soldier's neck as well. The cuffs concealed buttons that when undone allowed the soldier to roll the sleeves up. As the *Heer* generally wore decorations on *Feldblusen*, soldiers typically sewed loops on the left breast that allowed the mounting of ribbons and badges without damaging the material. Shoulder straps, either sewn on or buttoned on, completed the *Feldbluse*, which is often referred to as the 'M36'.

In 1939, GD's standard-issue *Steingrau* (stone grey) *Hose* (trousers) had provisions for both braces and a waist belt, and troops often wore both. The trousers had two front and two rear pockets, and the early 'M36' trousers also had a watch pocket and a ring to attach a fob. Trousers issued after 1940 were *Feldgrau* (field grey) in colour, with similar variations in shade as for the *Feldblusen*. Trousers produced from 1943 had a similar arrangement of pockets and belt loops, but were cut to be more accommodating to the new low boots which were becoming the standard footwear. The material quality of trousers also began its gradual decline.

As well as a spade in a leather carrier (folding spades were issued subsequently), each man was also issued with a bayonet, scabbard and frog; a bread bag in which he usually kept his toiletries, small personal items, shaving gear and some food; a canteen with Bakelite or metal cup; and a mess kit with lid, with the mess kit and canteen usually strapped to the bread bag. Troops also carried a gas mask stored in a metal canister with cleaning supplies and spare lenses. A gas cape was usually secured in a pouch to the outside of the gas-mask canister. This man's waist belt with enlisted man's buckle and rifle magazine pouches supports the bread bag on his right hip, with his canteen suspended from it; a gas-mask canister is suspended from a strap over his shoulder.

(4) Second-type GD *Ärmelstreifen*

GD personnel wearing *Mäntel* and gloves train alongside an early StuG III assault gun, probably in early 1941. Note how the dark uniforms and vehicle colour scheme stand out against the snow; winter conditions in Germany were not adequate preparation for winter campaigning in the Soviet Union. The early StuG III variant that was attached to GD during the battle of France utilized the short-barrelled 7.5cm StuK 37 gun, similar to the main armament of the PzKpfw IV medium tank. Subsequent versions were armed with the longer, more effective 7.5cm StuK 40, and one, later two, MG 34 machine guns. With a four-man crew, the StuG III was very mobile and could manage speeds up to 40km/h. The StuG III Ausf. A–D had 50mm of frontal armour, making them resistant to many anti-tank guns and all anti-tank rifles from the front except those extremely lucky shots that struck tracks, sensitive equipment or vision slits. (Süddeutsche Zeitung Photo/Alamy Stock Photo)

OPPOSITE
Swearing-in of recruits, 6 March 1941. Note the use of double-decal helmets. (Scherl/Süddeutsche Zeitung Photo/Alamy Stock Photo)

An SdKfz 10 prime mover tows a 3.7cm PaK anti-tank gun through the snow during training, 27 January 1941. Light, mobile and cost-effective, the 3.7cm PaK provided adequate firepower against light tanks and fortifications, but quickly became obsolete in the face of French, British and Soviet heavy armour. (Scherl/Süddeutsche Zeitung Photo/Alamy Stock Photo)

of war. Operations around the city of Lyon resulted in the surrender of that city on 19 June. On 20 June, following the surrender of a group of Senegalese soldiers at Chasselay, the prisoners were massacred by elements of IR (mot.) GD. On 25 June a ceasefire stopped all fighting in France.

Although GD trained tentatively for the invasion of Britain and then for operations against Gibraltar, these missions never took place. From September 1940, Artillerie-Abteilung 400 was attached to the regiment. Over the winter of 1940/41, IR (mot.) GD underwent a period of training and replacement to prepare for the invasion of the Soviet Union. In December, a fifth battalion was added, including motorcycle (17), *Pionier* (18), communications (19) and anti-aircraft (20) companies.

IR (mot.) GD participated in the invasion of Yugoslavia (6–18 April 1941), but saw very little combat action. Following the conclusion of the campaign, the regiment was again involved in an atrocity, this time at the village of Pančevo, where IR (mot.) GD personnel were involved in the executions of 36 civilians on 22 April.

OPERATION *BARBAROSSA*

During the course of Operation *Barbarossa*, IR (mot.) GD would fight in some of the fiercest engagements of 1941, and advance as far as Tula, just south of Moscow. Setting out from its billets south-east of Warsaw in the early morning of 25 June 1941, IR (mot.) GD moved into the Soviet Union as part of Heeresgruppe Mitte. The initial days of the invasion were heady for GD and Heeresgruppe Mitte. Although the Soviet Union had a massive establishment of forces on paper, the invasion caught them largely off guard and in a poor position to react properly to the invasion (Glantz 1999: 50–51). On 30 June, subordinated to Panzergruppe 2, the regiment was tasked with preventing a break-out from the encircled Soviet armies around Minsk, a role it carried out until 3 July, when it was ordered to move towards the Beresina River and beyond it, Smolensk.

OPPOSITE
A Heer officer with *Ärmelstreifen* points his sidearm at an executed prisoner during the Pančevo atrocity, Yugoslavia, 12 April 1941. The officer with *Schirmmütze* to his left appears to be a member of the SS. (ullstein bild/ullstein bild via Getty Images)

An 8cm Granatenwerfer 34 mortar crew. Offering superior accuracy, the GrW 34 lobbed a bomb almost 2.5km at its maximum eventual range. It could fire faster and was far less complicated to maintain than conventional artillery, being smoothbore. It was aimed using a method similar to surveying with a sight and aiming stakes, and it could adjust fire extremely quickly. GD's GrW 34 mortar crews used either smoke or high-explosive ammunition in their mortars. Germany developed a bounding round that bounced back into the air after impact but before detonation, creating a lethal air burst without the gunners having to spend time meticulously adjusting fuzes. Many of GD's mortar crewmen would find themselves sharing most if not all the dangers of the riflemen, and there was considerable mutual respect between them. (Nik Cornish at www.stavka.org.uk)

Soon, the casualties began to mount noticeably for IR (mot.) GD and for the Wehrmacht. On 11 July, IR (mot.) GD was placed under command of the 10. Panzer-Division and ordered to attack across the Dnepr River towards Yelnya. Throughout the day, elements of the regiment crossed under fire and the *Pioniere* were able to bridge the river despite Soviet counter-attacks. Vicious, if often ill-coordinated counter-attacks combined with bad roads and challenging terrain including formidable obstacles such as the Dnepr, slowly bled away German strength and challenged German logistics.

German troops seized part of Smolensk on 16 July. The tenacious and massive Soviet counter-attacks near Smolensk beginning in late July gave the men of IR (mot.) GD a taste of defensive fighting, often conducted at night. August brought similar defensive missions, as the German forces moved further into the Soviet Union. Only on 18 August was the regiment relieved and able to recover from the ordeal of combat. An award ceremony on 25 August saw Oberleutnant Karl Hänert, commander of 4./IR (mot.) GD, become the first member of the regiment serving in the Soviet Union to receive the *Ritterkreuz* (Knight's Cross), in recognition of his efforts during the defensive battles around Yelnya.

On 30 August, IR (mot.) GD was ordered to depart for Ukraine. September and October 1941 saw the regiment involved in the Axis effort to capture the city of Kiev in the teeth of stubborn Soviet resistance. Relieved on 3 October, the regiment then prepared for the operation against Moscow, *Typhoon*, now critically delayed due to interference and shifting priorities. As the fighting wore on into the winter, the troops were exhausted, logistics

B OPERATION *BARBAROSSA*, 1941

This scene shows an MG 34 machine-gun team in action, emplaced behind a dirt berm. The standard German machine gun in 1941, the MG 34 was manufactured until the end of World War II, although the MG 42 began to replace it from 1942 onwards. Man-portable and air-cooled, the MG 34 typically fired about 800rd/min. It could be employed in the medium or heavy role by attaching it to a tripod and could also be fitted with an optical sight. In addition, an anti-aircraft tripod was standard issue and usually carried in platoon, company or headquarters trains; and most machine-gunners carried an anti-aircraft sight, giving German infantrymen on-the-spot defence against low-flying enemy aircraft. Two Stielhandgranaten 24 (stick grenades) and an Eihandgranate 39 (egg grenade) are at hand should close-quarter combat ensue.

(1) *Unteroffizier*

The NCO wears a single-decal helmet with looped chinstrap; his M41 *Feldbluse* bears NCO *Tresse* and he displays the *EK II* ribbon in his second buttonhole. The *Feldbluse* was simplified during the course of 1940–41, resulting in what collectors and enthusiasts refer to as the 'M41'. The bottle-green facing cloth on the collar was omitted and it now matched the remainder of the garment. The interior and exterior were basically identical otherwise.

Standard infantry equipment is worn, including the right-side three-magazine pouch issued for the MP 40 submachine gun and the rolled *Zeltbahn*, a camouflaged shelter-quarter which doubled as a rain poncho. The shelter-quarter had a light side and a dark side, both of which were printed in standard *Splittertarn* (splinter pattern). Constructed of a heavy duck, the material was remarkably waterproof, and its concealment capabilities were also appreciated. Most men also carried a very handy small alcohol stove with Esbit solid-fuel tablets, and a *Göffel* or 'spork' folding spoon-and-fork combination.

He has inserted a knife into the magazine pouch for personal defence. Up to six MP 40 magazines could be carried in a pair of three-cell magazine pouches with one magazine in the weapon. Featuring a small pocket on the side for a loading tool, these pouches were most commonly made out of linen, and ran the gamut of colours from a medium green to khaki-tan. In addition, six-magazine pouches were also issued in limited numbers, especially to assault units such as *Sturmpioniere*, although it is unclear whether any of these magazine pouches saw service with GD personnel.

(2) *Schütze*

The private soldier firing an MG 34 machine gun is squinting through the optic while squeezing the solenoid trigger with his right hand. His minimal belt gear includes the machine-gunner's magazine pouch on his right hip.

(3) *Schütze*

Bringing up ammunition in four battered ammunition tins – two in each hand – this stooped soldier has slung his Kar 98k rifle over his back.

(4) Enlisted man's *Schulterklappe*

The enlisted man's shoulder strap featured the unit monogram and was piped in white. As the unit expanded and incorporated other arms of service, other colours were used for monogram and piping.

were stretched beyond their limits, the equipment that remained was worn out, and finally, the cold became almost unbearable (Glantz 1999: 184–92). Oberleutnant Hänert was one of many casualties, killed in action on 14 October. IR (mot.) GD's advance ended before Tula, south of Moscow, and well short of the goal. On 5 December, the Soviet forces unleashed an offensive that pushed the regiment and the rest of the Wehrmacht well away from Moscow with fresh troops, many from Siberia (Spaeter 1992: 265). From 23 December, the regiment bolstered German defences along the Oka River, fighting from makeshift positions blasted out of the frozen ground as the temperature fell to -30°C.

Oberstleutnant Alfred Greim, commander of II./IR (mot.) GD, wears the officer's *Feldmütze* with arm-of-service *Soutache*. He was awarded the *RK* in recognition of his leadership during the successful defence of the western bank of the Upa River on 13 December 1941. His medals include the *Ehrenzeichen des 9. November 1923*, aka the *Blutorden*, above the *Deutsches Kreuz in Gold* on his right breast pocket; the *Infanterie-Sturmabzeichen* is below the *EK I* on his left breast pocket. On 19 May 1943, Greim died of blood poisoning in hospital at Döberitz, Germany. (Bundesarchiv, Bild 101I-748-0090-15A/Kempe/ CC-BY-SA 3.0 de)

A motorcyclist of IR (mot.) GD wears the *Feldmütze* with goggles; note the GD unit insignia on the vehicle behind him. (Nik Cornish at www.stavka.org.uk)

OPERATIONS IN 1942

The first days of 1942 saw more defensive fighting, with IR (mot.) GD going over to the attack on 8 February. Combat losses prompted Oberst Walter Hörnlein to merge I. and II./IR (mot.) GD into a single rifle battalion under the command of Major Kurt Gehrke. Only when replacements arrived on 28 February could some troops be rested and the two separate battalions re-formed. The regiment remained in the line until 9 April, by which time Hörnlein had been promoted to *Generalmajor* and the expansion of the unit to divisional status had been announced.

The Infanterie-Division (mot.) 'Großdeutschland' fielded two infantry regiments, initially designated '1' and '2', each with three rifle battalions and a support battalion. Infanterie-Regiment (mot.) GD 2 was raised on 20 March 1942. Artillerie-Abteilung (mot.) 400 became the I. Abteilung of a new Artillerie-Regiment GD. The division also had a reconnaissance battalion, Kradschützen-Bataillon GD, formed on 1 March; a three-company assault-gun battalion, Sturmgeschütz-Abteilung GD, formed on 4 April from Sturmgeschütz-Abteilung 192 and 16./IR (mot.) GD; a three-company tank battalion, Panzer-Abteilung GD, formerly I./PzRgt 100, redesignated on 5 February; an anti-aircraft battalion, FlaK-Artillerie-Abteilung GD; an anti-tank battalion, Panzerjäger-Abteilung GD; a signals battalion, Nachrichten-Abteilung GD; and the usual array of divisional support units.

By mid-May 1942, ID (mot.) GD was ready for action, all elements except the newly renamed IR (mot.) GD 1 having being brought together at the Wandern training ground (Spaeter 1992: 294–99). In late May the division returned to the Eastern Front, halting in Poland to give the recruits field experience before moving further east to join the XXXXVIII. Panzerkorps near the Don River. On 4 June, Oberstleutnant Alfred Greim, the commander of II./IR (mot.) GD 1, was awarded the *Ritterkreuz* in recognition of his leadership during the defensive battles on 13 December, as was Oberleutnant Peter Frantz of StuGAbt GD on 12 June.

By 27 June, IR (mot.) GD was in position, ready for the start of the planned offensive at 0215hrs on 28 June. Following the German bombardment, IR (mot.) GD 2 and elements of PzBtl GD, both units making their combat debut, attacked the fortified village of Dubrovka,

A Gew 41(W) semi-automatic rifle. While most infantry continued to field the Kar 98k, the Gew 41 was issued to GD beginning in early 1942, though small numbers may have made their way to the division earlier. There were two versions of the Gew 41, one made by Walther, the Gew 41(W), and one made by Mauser, the Gew 41(M). The Walther-made rifle was far simpler and produced in much greater numbers, and GD's troops seem to have been issued these exclusively. Utilizing a gas-trap system instead of a piston, the Gew 41(W) was fed by standard Kar 98k five-round stripper clips into a fixed ten-round internal box magazine. GD's infantrymen equipped with the Gew 41(W) found the rifle to be well-made, but temperamental. It needed to be cleaned meticulously, and the gas system and ammunition combined to create almost instant fouling and carbon build-up that required constant attention, even in an army renowned for its emphasis on weapons maintenance. Although it developed an unfortunate reputation for stoppages and was clearly not the solution GD's riflemen needed in the Soviet Union's harsh climatic conditions, the Gew 41(W) was an accurate weapon; at least some were fitted with telescopic sights, although this seems to have been a rarity, and the author has never found evidence of GD usage of such sighted weapons in photographs, recollections or histories. (Armémuseum (The Swedish Army Museum)/Wikimedia/CC BY-SA 4.0)

which had been laid waste by the German artillery and aerial onslaught. III./IR (mot.) GD 2 was tasked with initiating the pursuit and capturing the bridges over the Tim River, with I./IR (mot.) GD 2 in support. Having seized the rail bridge over the Tim intact, the lead elements of IR (mot.) GD 2 were hit by friendly fire from Luftwaffe bombers, with Major Ludwig Kohlhaas, the battalion commander, being wounded and handing command to Hauptmann Prüss; Kohlhaas subsequently received the *Ritterkreuz* for his part in the capture of the bridge. KradBtl GD took the lead, reaching Nikolaevo.

On 29 June the dry weather gave way to heavy rain, making it difficult for the vehicles to get traction. Elements of IR (mot.) GD 1 established a bridgehead across the Kshen River and by the evening had reached Alexandrovka; by the evening of 30 June the Olym River had also been crossed, leaving ID (mot.) GD's leading elements deep in enemy territory.

During the evening of 4 July, Oberleutnant Carl-Ludwig Blumenthal, commander of 7./IR (mot.) GD 1, seized and held the crucial Semiluki road bridge over the Don River, allowing the division's leading elements to continue their advance. Blumenthal was awarded the *Ritterkreuz* on 18 September. The German advance continued, with the major city of Voronezh their target; elements of I./IR (mot.) GD 1 aboard the assault guns of StuGAbt GD were the first German troops to enter the city, on 5 July. By the evening of 6 July, the exhausted troops of ID (mot.) GD had carved out a substantial bridgehead within the city.

There was no respite in July, as ID (mot.) GD was ordered south, with KradBtl GD in the lead. The pace of the advance could only be sustained by fuel drops from Luftwaffe aircraft. The leading elements of the division crossed the Donets River on 20 July before capturing Kerchik and going on to cross the Don on 22 July. The various units of the division were pulled out of the line in early August, but instead of heading for France as had been hoped, the men of ID (mot.) GD were ordered to Smolensk, arriving in stages from 17 August.

From 9 September, ID (mot.) GD was involved in some of the heaviest and bloodiest fighting of 1942, at Rzhev. Cities such as Kiev had been fought over during 1941, but the struggles in places such as Rzhev and Stalingrad defined the *Rattenkrieg* or 'War of the Rats', fought street to street, in the sewers, room to room, floor to floor, and very often under conditions of close combat. In these conditions tanks were at a disadvantage and the infantry and *Pioniere* took the lead. While the Soviet forces had often fought hard, IR (mot.) GD experienced the growing abilities of the partially renewed Soviet armed forces

C

EASTERN FRONT, 1942

(1) *Oberschütze*, June 1942

This soldier on the march has his Kar 98k rifle equipped with a Zielfernrohr 41 (ZF41) telescopic sight resting on his shoulder. He wears the 'M42' *Feldmütze* with eagle and cockade but no *Soutache*. Appearing in 1942, the short-lived M42 *Feldmütze* resembled the earlier M38 *Feldmütze* except that it had ear flaps that could be pulled over the ears in cold weather and fixed by two small buttons at the front. This cap seems to have remained in production maybe as late as late 1943 or early 1944, but examples are scarce, and they are not commonly depicted in photographs.

A single-decal Stahlhelm 40 hangs from his right front Kar 98k magazine pouch. The Stahlhelm 40 did away with the multi-piece vents found on the Stahlhelm 35. Until 1940 the helmet sported both the national tricolour and the Heer eagle. Beginning in 1941, the Heer eagle only was retained and as the war progressed *Stahlhelme* were often issued with no decals. Colours again varied, but earlier helmets usually had an apple-green finish with later examples sporting a darker shade of field grey, often painted over the earlier apple green, creating an interesting contrast as the paint wore off. Troops frequently attached rubber bands or their bread-bag straps to the helmet to enable the fixing of foliage for camouflage.

His M41 *Feldbluse*, the cuffs unbuttoned and the sleeves rolled up, has the mid-war GD cuff title on the right sleeve and a rank pip on the left arm (not visible). His identification disc is visible at his throat. He wears the *Eisernes Kreuz 2. Klasse* (EK II: Iron Cross 2nd Class) and *Ostmedaille* (Winter Battle in the East 1941–42 Medal aka Eastern Medal) ribbons in his second buttonhole, and the *Verwundetenabzeichen in Schwarz* (Wound Badge in Black) and *Infanterie-Sturmabzeichen* (Infantry Assault Badge) on his left breast pocket. His standard rifleman's equipment includes a set of leather braces or 'Y-straps' that helped support the weight of the belt.

(2) *Oberst*, autumn 1942

This colonel wears the 'crusher'-style peaked cap with white infantry piping, and goggles, with officer's M36 tunic and legwear. His decorations include the *Ritterkreuz*, worn at the neck; the *Eisernes Kreuz 1. Klasse* with *Spange* (EK I; Iron Cross 1st Class with Clasp) on his left breast pocket, along with the *Infanterie-Sturmabzeichen*, the *Verwundetenabzeichen in Silber* and a *Deutsches Sportabzeichen* (German Sports Badge) *in Bronze*; and the World War I EK II with 1939 *Spange* and *Ostmedaille* ribbons in his second buttonhole. He wears a map case on his left hip, with his pistol holster worn on his right side.

(3) *Schütze*, December 1942

Armed with a Kar 98k rifle, this heavily bundled infantryman is wearing as many layers as possible beneath his M40 *Mantel* (greatcoat). His whitewashed Stahlhelm 40 bears no insignia. He wears several standard-issue toques (tube scarves) around his neck and head. His winter gloves have the standard white rings around the wrist indicating the size.

During the winter of 1941/42, the greatcoat issued to most men and carried by most officers did not provide enough protection from the extreme cold encountered in the Soviet Union. Although the Heer issued sweaters and gloves, these were also found to be inadequate. While troops frequently piled on as many scarves and toques as they could find, in addition to socks and gloves, frostbite was a serious problem over the winter of 1941/42, and men frequently lost fingers, toes and other extremities to the elements.

Like all soldiers, some of GD's men had additional clothing sent from home or they scrounged it as they could. They found that the Soviet troops' padded suits, felt boots and fur hats were remarkably effective in thwarting the cold. Further, the hobnailed *Marschstiefel* were found to be a detriment, as the hobnails transmitted the extreme cold straight into the boot. Made of rope, this man's 'Sentry Shoes' are worn over his *Marschstiefel*. Although German troops were issued winter boots after 1941, most GD soldiers had hobnails in their boots throughout the war, and in places like the Soviet Union, cold injuries to feet continued to be an issue until 1945.

Beginning in the autumn of 1942, many new types of cold-weather clothing became available, and GD, as an elite unit, got some of the first examples. The basic overcoat design was modified for sentry duty with the addition of a taller collar and fur lining. By the winter of 1942/43, German troops began to be issued with specialized winter footwear. The most outlandish of these designs were rope boots for sentries that were designed to slip on and off over the standard-issue jackboots or the lace-up low boots that began to appear in quantity during 1942. Rope boots were completely unsuited for walking long distances, but they were excellent insulators in extreme cold and undoubtedly kept many GD sentries from losing their toes.

In addition, GD personnel were issued some of the new winter boots adapted in design from the Russian felt boots captured during the first winter of the war on the Eastern Front. These boots had somewhat conventional leather soles, but were lined with thick wool felt that was a superb insulator. In addition, the construction meant the soldier could move normally, unlike with the rope boots, which were only useful if the soldier intended to remain stationary.

(4) Mid-war officer's *Ärmelstreifen*

GD personnel in a *Kübelwagen*, the versatile light utility vehicle designed by Ferdinand Porsche and manufactured by Volkswagen, May 1942. Note the MG 34 held by the man in the back seat, and the straps affixed to the men's helmets. (ullstein bild/ullstein bild via Getty Images)

for the first time around Rzhev, as the flailing mass attacks of 1941 gave way to more coordinated combined-arms attacks. Soviet artillery began to improve as well, and the combined effort decimated GD's front-line strength, with already depleted units dwindling even further (Spaeter 1992: 397).

ID (mot.) GD's *Sturmpioniere* played an important part in clearing Soviet bunkers and fortifications at close quarters in built-up and fortified areas south of Rzhev, pushing Soviet forces out of key positions and eliminating dozens of bunkers and fighting positions in fighting that earned Oberleutnant Horst Warschnauer the *Ritterkreuz* for the actions of his men on 22 September. On 30 September one of IR (mot.) GD's earliest *Ritterkreuz* recipients, Oberst Garski, was killed in action leading his men from the front (Spaeter 1992: 412–17). On that same day, Unteroffizier Hans Klemm of 2./ IR (mot.) GD 1 won the *Ritterkreuz* for his initiative and daring after his company commander was killed.

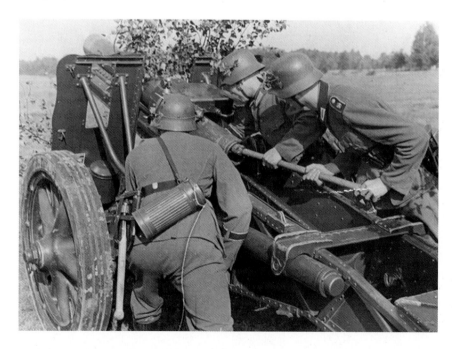

A GD crew at work with a 15cm sIG 33 infantry gun, 1942. From the outset, GD had companies equipped with light and heavy infantry guns that directly supported its efforts. The 7.5cm leichtes Infanteriegeschütz 18 (leIG 18) and 15cm schwere Infanteriegeschütz 33 (sIG 33) were in many cases used in the direct-fire role, although both were capable of indirect fire. Weighing only 400kg, the leIG 18 was easy to manoeuvre and position, with a range of 3,550m and a rate of fire of 8–12rd/min, while the 1.8-tonne sIG 33 could fire high-explosive or smoke rounds – and later, hollow-charge and demolition rounds – at a rate of 2–3rd/min and a range of up to 4,700m. (Bundesarchiv, Bild 146-2006-0057/CC-BY-SA 3.0 de)

RK-winner Oberleutnant Peter Frantz is borne aloft by his men. Frantz won the RK on 4 June 1942 as an *Oberleutnant* in command of 16./IR (mot.) GD and the *Eichenlaub* on 14 April 1943 as a *Hauptmann* in command of StuGAbt GD. (Süddeutsche Zeitung Photo/Alamy Stock Photo)

At the beginning of October, GD was pulled out of the line again, and sent to rest and refit (Spaeter 1992: 427–32). GD truly earned its *Feuerwehr* ('fire brigade') moniker during the fighting in the Luchesa Valley. Dispersed and depleted elements of IR (mot.) GD – including a temporary ski battalion, formed on 28 October – were placed in the line at various places in the Luchesa Valley to act as 'stiffeners' for other depleted and less well-equipped German units (Buttar 2020: 321–23). Although ID (mot.) GD was employed piecemeal through the length of the valley, it was expected to remain effective, and the division's *ésprit de corps* endured despite heavy casualties. Many of the division's elements were reduced to less than 50 per cent of their existing strengths during this fighting. Massed Soviet armoured attacks were dealt with using a combination of handheld mines and charges, 8.8cm anti-aircraft guns from various units and what inherent

Generalmajor Walter Hörnlein is pictured with GD StuG crews, June 1942; the officer to his left, Oberleutnant Peter Frantz, has just been awarded the RK. An RK winner himself in July 1941, Hörnlein led IR (mot.) GD from August 1941 until ID (mot.) GD was formed in April 1942, when he assumed command of the division. He led GD until January 1944, subsequently commanding the LXXXII. Armeekorps and latterly the XXVII. Armeekorps, and ending the war as a *General der Infanterie*. (Bundesarchiv, Bild 101I-748-0090-03A/Kempe/CC-BY-SA 3.0 de)

Pictured in 1942 or 1943, these GD troops are gathered in a *Schützenpanzerwagen* (armoured personnel carrier). The smoking man wears a *Panzerjacke*. (INTERFOTO/Alamy Stock Photo)

anti-tank guns the division had remaining, mostly 5cm PaK 38 guns that were often of little use against the T-34 tank in the frontal arc except at extremely close range. On 1 December, Oberst Otto Köhler, the commander of GrenRgt GD, was killed by a mortar round. He was succeeded by Major Karl Lorenz, who was awarded the *Ritterkreuz* on 17 December in recognition of his decisive leadership in the face of imminent disaster for the regiment.

In the closing weeks of 1942, as Soviet forces strove to envelop Stalingrad, a contingent from the Führer-Begleit-Bataillon (FBB) commanded by Hauptmann Wilhelm Pohlmann was rushed to the front line. It played a key role in stemming the Red Army's advance and aiding the beleaguered German forces to retreat and thereby evade capture or destruction.

D **FALL BLAU, 1942**
This scene shows three GD soldiers engaged in street fighting.
(1) Unteroffizier
This slightly wounded infantry NCO, holding a Stielhandgranate 24 in his right hand, is pulling the ceramic bead to ignite the grenade fuze. His MP 40 submachine gun with stock extended is slung over his shoulder. He wears a Stahlhelm 40 with a rubber band around it for attaching foliage. The sleeves of his M41 *Feldbluse* are rolled up; note the NCO *Tresse*. His decorations include the *EK II* and *Ostmedaille* ribbons in his second buttonhole and the *Infanterie-Sturmabzeichen* on his left breast pocket. In preparation for close combat, he has tucked an entrenching tool into his standard enlisted man's gear with MP 40 magazine pouches.
(2) Schütze
His Kar 98k rifle slung, this private soldier readies a *Geballte Ladung* (concentrated charge). He wears a Stahlhelm 40, M41

Feldbluse and standard-issue legwear, with a close-combat knife inserted in his boot. His regulation equipment omits the leather Y-straps.
(3) Schütze
This soldier holds a captured Soviet PPSh-41 submachine gun, with the magazine pouch visible on his right hip. Although pistols, rifles and machine guns captured from occupied countries were often issued to German troops, GD continued to be lavishly equipped with the best Germany had to offer throughout World War II, and GD's troops were mostly issued with German-produced weapons. Captured Soviet small arms were utilized in small quantities by GD's troops, perhaps as early as 1941, but evidence suggests that by 1942 this was still by no means common. The commonest captured Soviet small arms in use included the PPSh-41 and the SVT-40 self-loading rifle. Both of these weapons were simple, reliable and effective, especially the PPSh-41, which endured the harshest conditions and delivered 1,200rd/min in most circumstances.

This GD soldier has a *Schiessbecher* (grenade launcher) mounted on his Kar 98k rifle, June 1943. Depending upon time, space and mission, one man per platoon usually carried a grenade launcher. This allowed the rifle platoon indirect-fire capacity and a limited high-explosive and anti-tank capacity, especially as new ammunition was developed throughout World War II. The grenade launcher was milled and rifled, and the grenade was inserted from the front and seated tightly to the base. The launcher itself fitted over the muzzle of the rifle and was secured with a clamp, and was carried in a leather pouch along with a sight, a level and a wrench for disassembly, adjustment and cleaning. (Bundesarchiv, Bild 101I-732-0123-15/Pfeiffer/ CC-BY-SA 3.0 de)

OPPOSITE
Pictured in early 1943, Oberst Hyazinth Graf Strachwitz von Gross Zauche und Kaminietz wears the *Panzerjacke* and an interesting winter version of the officer's *Feldmütze*. A World War I veteran who led armoured units with distinction in Poland, France, the Balkans and the Soviet Union, Strachwitz was given command of the newly formed PzRgt GD on 15 January 1943, leading the regiment in battle at Kursk until he was seriously injured on 10 July. He subsequently commanded a battlegroup on the Eastern Front, winning the *Ritterkreuz mit Eichenlaub, Schwerten und Brillanten* on 15 April, and was again severely wounded, ending the war as a *Generalmajor*. (Heinrich Hoffmann/ullstein bild via Getty Images)

OPERATIONS IN 1943

Defensive operations continued into the first days of 1943, when it seemed as though ID (mot.) GD was heading for Stalingrad (Spaeter 1995: 9). In the event, however, advance elements of the division left Smolensk on 15 January, bound for Kupyansk on the Oskol River. The first sub-unit to reach the front line was I./FüsRgt GD, occupying positions at Volokonovka on 19 January, followed two days later by I./GrenRgt GD, detraining near Volchansk. As the division gathered its strength it was quickly involved in defensive fighting against superior numbers of Soviet troops. On 14 March 1943, Hauptmann Pohlmann was awarded the *Ritterkreuz* in recognition of his leadership during operations around the city of Belgorod in mid-January.

Once the newly redesignated AufklAbt GD arrived, ID (mot.) GD was able to gain a more effective appreciation of the enemy forces it faced. The leading elements of the division distinguished themselves in combined-arms combat during the first days of February, covering the withdrawal of Axis forces from Belgorod. The brutal and prolonged fighting that ensued saw the German forces conduct a gruelling retreat in the face of repeated attacks. During this period, prominent members of the division such as Oberstleutnant Karl Lorenz, commander of GrenRgt GD, and his subordinate Hauptmann Otto Ernst Remer distinguished themselves in battle. The fighting was extremely confused, with local attacks and counter-attacks frequently resulting in mini-encirclements on both sides (Spaeter 1995: 32).

As ID (mot.) GD withdrew slowly toward the northern edge of Kharkov, it destroyed bridges and left mines in its wake, turning as opportunities allowed to deliver sharp blows designed to keep the Soviet forces at a distance and give evacuating troops to the south time to escape. The city of Kharkov was abandoned and recaptured by Soviet forces on 16 February. By 24 February, the division was fighting alongside elements of Waffen-SS divisions in the area, presaging their cooperation later in 1943 (Spaeter 1995: 56). The weather continued to be challenging, with thaws in early to mid-

March resulting in mud that limited mobility and created greater fuel and supply problems than those usually experienced.

The German counter-attack at Kharkov in March resembled Axis operations early in *Barbarossa*. The Soviet forces had become overextended and their capture of Kharkov created a prominent salient in the German line, with ID (mot.) GD situated on the northern side. On 7 March, the German counter-attack made rapid progress; although the participating elements of the division and the Waffen-SS units were understrength, they still had considerable potential offensive power. By mid-March, GD had endured six months of fighting with very little rest. The heavy fighting saw several awards of the *Ritterkreuz*, with Generalleutnant Hörnlein being awarded the *Eichenlaub* (Oak Leaves) on 15 March (Spaeter 1995: 76), the day Kharkov fell to German forces once again.

E. *PIONIERE* IN OPERATION *ZITADELLE*, 1943

(1) *Pionier*

Wearing an M43 *Feldbluse* with black branch-of-service piping and GD cipher on the *Schulterklappen*, this *Pionier* is armed with an FmW 41, which joined the earlier FmW 35 in front-line service. Projecting a stream of burning fuel oil 35–50m, the FmW 35 was effective against bunkers, emplacements and even tanks. Although specialized protective equipment was available for flamethrower teams, it seems to have never or at least very rarely been worn in combat.

(2) *Feldwebel*

About to fit a fresh magazine to his MP 40 submachine gun, this *Pionier Feldwebel* wears a reversible splinter-pattern smock and helmet cover; a close-combat knife is tucked into the smock between the laces. Beginning in 1943, GD began to receive an increasing quantity of camouflage uniforms. At first, the most commonly issued camouflage pattern was *Splittertarn*, the same pattern that appeared on the *Zeltbahn*. This was used on both helmet covers and smocks, both of which began to be well-represented in GD before Kursk. The smock was designed as an overgarment that was supposed to disrupt the silhouette of the soldier and make him harder to spot under battlefield conditions. They were produced using a variety of materials, and in different base shades from a sort of light grey to medium and even lighter tans, with blocky geometric shapes in brown and green with small 'splinters' of green that ran through the pattern. The outside of the smock had a lace-up neck, and cuffs that could be taken in in most models with a strap at the wrist and a series of buttons. Some smocks were reversible to white, and others were not. Two slant pockets allowed the wearer some access to the *Feldbluse*.

The splinter-pattern helmet cover simply slipped over the helmet and was secured with a drawstring. There were loops to attach foliage and other camouflage materials. Some of them were also reversible to white. Helmet covers were subjected to a great amount of wear, especially with the flared-rim Stahlhelm 42, and surviving examples are fairly rare. There is ample evidence they were issued in some quantity to members of GD from 1943 onward. Priority seems to have given to infantrymen and *Pioniere* in the issue of both smocks and helmet covers.

(3) *Pionier*

Armed with a Kar 98k rifle, this heavily laden *Pionier* is equipped with a complete set of assault bags (left and right) and backpack for *Pioniere*, plus the usual bread bag with attached canteen at the right rear. He wears an M43 tunic and trousers with low boots, and short-button gaiters. Issued from 1942, low boots were an indication of the pressure on Germany's war economy. They were basic leather boots that rose slightly above the ankle and had a lace-up front. Like the jackboot, these were hobnailed and most had toe caps and heel plates over leather soles. While many viewed the low boots as a poor substitute, they had a number of advantages. They were much easier to put on or take off, the laces could be loosened or tightened for comfort, and the leather was of generally good quality (until towards the end of the war) and could be well polished and reasonably waterproofed.

His Stahlhelm 42, omitting the folded-under rim found on previous models, has bread-bag straps attached. As GD's troops began to be issued the Stahlhelm 42 it initially retained the single Heer eagle decal. In time, this decal was also eliminated and the helmet was simply issued in a grey-green finish with sand mixed in to dull the tone and shine as matt paint was not yet in production. It was increasingly common for troops in 1942 onward to apply some sort of camouflage finish to their helmets with available paint. Although in the beginning this was mostly done with white paint in the winter, greens, tans, browns and other earth tones became more common as the war progressed. After issued camouflage helmet covers became more common later in the war, the flared edges of the Stahlhelm 42 frequently wore out the edges of the helmet cover faster as Heer helmet covers did not have rocker clips like those issued to the Waffen-SS. There was one final attempt to improve the *Stahlhelm*, which resulted in the Stahlhelm 45; but there is no evidence suggesting GD was issued this helmet.

(4) Mid-war enlisted man's *Schulterklappe, Pioniere*

GD's *Schulterklappen* had the GD cipher embroidered for the enlisted man, generally in the same colour as the branch-of-service piping. Thus, enlisted men in the infantry had white ciphers with white piping on the edges of the *Schulterklappen*, artillery had red ciphers with red piping, and so on. As GD expanded, the number of colours and types expanded as well. GD's insignia did not all come from the same manufacturer and there are multiple examples of original insignia that are not quite identical. There are variations in the colour and shape of ciphers and other details.

In late March, ID (mot.) GD finally withdrew for refitting. On 3 April, Generalleutnant Hermann Balck took command of the division, and on 19 May it was converted into a *Panzergrenadier-Division*, which fundamentally altered its structure, increased its complement of troops and massively expanded its firepower and capabilities. Operation *Zitadelle*, the German offensive to eliminate the Kursk salient, was originally scheduled for May, but it was delayed until July primarily so units such as PzGrenDiv GD and the Waffen-SS divisions could receive some of the newest equipment. Tank units subordinated to PzGrenDiv GD during *Zitadelle* were equipped with the new PzKpfw V 'Panther' medium tank, Germany's answer to the Soviet T-34; but the Panther's combat debut would reveal it to have many faults that needed to be remedied. The division was also equipped with the legendary PzKpfw VI 'Tiger' tank, a type already familiar to Soviet forces.

GD's infantrymen, gunners and *Pioniere* were also thoroughly resupplied during March–June in preparation for *Zitadelle*. At the beginning of June, Remer's I./PzGrenRgt GD received 83 SdKfz 251 armoured personnel carriers (Spaeter 1995: 89). The division seems to have shed the last of its 5cm PaK 38 guns before Kursk and fielded only 7.5cm PaK 40 guns during *Zitadelle*.

As part of Heeresgruppe Süd and the XLVIII. Panzerkorps, PzGrenDiv GD was to operate in the most concentrated area of German armour to participate in *Zitadelle*. Immediately to the east of the XLVIII. Panzerkorps, the II. SS-Panzerkorps, which included the 1., 2. and 3. SS-Panzergrenadier-Divisionen, operated in close conjunction. This armour heavy grouping was to strike north, in theory eventually meeting up with units from the 9. Panzerarmee striking southwards. Although the city of Kursk, situated

in the centre of the salient, was an aiming point, and gave its name to the battle, GD's command and soldiers understood that successful operations often required a considerable degree of flexibility.

During the afternoon of 4 July both of PzGrenDiv GD's infantry regiments were tasked with launching a surprise attack to capture a hill held by the Red Army and offering a commanding view of the German build-up. At 1500hrs on 4 July both III./PzGrenRgt GD (on the right) and III./PzFüsRgt GD (on the left), supported by StuG III assault guns, self-propelled anti-tank guns and *Sturmpioniere*, commenced their attack in heavy rain, with armoured observation vehicles of the division's artillery regiment zigzagging across the battlefield to avoid Soviet artillery fire. While both attacking battalions achieved their objectives at the cost of heavy casualties, the commander of III./PzFüsRgt GD, Hauptmann Siegfried Leyck, was mortally wounded; he was posthumously awarded the *Ritterkreuz* on 17 December 1943.

PzGrenDiv GD's preparations were offset by a slight shift in its lines before the attack on 5 July. The division's *Pioniere* worked at the Sisyphean task of clearing mines in the attack lanes, but were well aware they would not be able to get them all and keeping up the tempo of the attack meant taking risks. Part of those risks also included being somewhat uncertain as to the terrain in front of the division, a problem that persisted throughout *Zitadelle* for most German units (Spaeter 1995: 113). The depth and strength of Soviet defences at Kursk were immense. There were multiple belts that incorporated mines, anti-tank guns, anti-aircraft guns, tanks, infantry and extremely heavy concentrations of artillery. Once one belt was penetrated, the division's troops simply encountered another one (Glantz & House 1999: 64).

GD troops aboard a StuG III with the longer 7.5cm main gun, Kursk, July 1943. The fact that all of the soldiers are bareheaded places this scene behind the front line. (ullstein bild/ullstein bild via Getty Images)

PzGrenDiv GD's attack ran into problems from the beginning. The lack of information concerning the terrain ahead of the division drastically reduced the efficacy of its efforts. The herculean efforts of the *Pioniere* to clear mines were seemingly non-stop and around the clock; and often conducted under very heavy fire, resulting in serious casualties, including Oberst Erich Kahsnitz, the commander of PzFüsRgt GD, who was severely wounded; awarded the *Eichenlaub* for his efforts on 5 July, he died on 29 July. Oberstleutnant Karl-Anton Graf von Saurma-Jeltsch, brother-in-law of Oberst Hyazinth Graf Strachwitz and commander of II./PzRgt GD, was also seriously wounded on 5 July and died on 10 August.

The new Panther tanks, serving alongside the division's Panzer regiment under Graf Strachwitz – the 'Panzer Count', an extremely interesting and eccentric, but remarkably effective commander, and recipient of the *Ritterkreuz* – encountered difficulties from the outset. On 5 July, the Panthers cleared the jump-off point with relative ease, but soon ran into a swamp they had no idea was there; most got caught in the muck and missed much of the action during

F GD TROOPS, 1943

(1) *Leutnant*, Panzer-Regiment GD

With a pair of 10×50 binoculars suspended around his neck, this young tank commander wears the officer's *Feldmütze* with pink *Soutache*, the *Panzerjacke* (tank crewmen's double-breasted jacket) with mid-war cuff title, and standard-issue trousers for tank crewmen. Although berets were worn early in World War II, they were short-lived. A small number of experimental helmets for Panzer crewmen seem to have been made, and standard *Stahlhelme* might have been modified, but in general, helmets were rarely, if ever worn inside the tank, although crews would have been issued a variety of standard helmets and stowed them. Instead, tank crewmen wore the various iterations of the *Feldmütze* in black. Surviving photographs often show Panzer officers wearing the *Schirmmütze* (peaked cap) in field grey with pink piping.

His decorations include the *Panzerkampfabzeichen* (Tank Combat Badge) *in Silber*, the *EK I* and the *Verwundetenabzeichen in Silber* on his left breast and the *EK II* ribbon in his buttonhole. His officer's 'two post' belt supports a hard-shell P 38 pistol holster on his left hip.

(2) *Füsilier*, Füsilier-Regiment GD

This young infantryman carries an MG 42 machine gun on his right shoulder. His personal equipment includes the enlisted man's waist belt with machine-gun toolkit on his right hip and a soft-shell P 38 pistol holster on his left hip.

Entering GD service in 1942, the MG 42 utilized an advanced roller-locking design that allowed for a high rate of fire but also made the weapon extremely reliable in the harshest conditions including freezing temperatures. The MG 42 was simpler to produce than the MG 34, and the looser tolerances contributed to its increased reliability. In addition, the machine-gunner could change barrels faster as the barrel could simply be released to drop free of the weapon with the flick of a lever. While the standard quoted rate of fire for the MG 42 was 1,200rd/min, some managed 1,500rd/min without modification. GD's machine-gunners found the high rate of fire useful in the assault, but also in defence as their Soviet opponents almost always outnumbered them. A wide range

of accessories were available for the MG 42, including tripods and optics. A typical GD machine-gun team consisted of three men: one firing the weapon, one primarily responsible for reloading, and one directing and assisting. The machine gun was the core of the German infantry unit and its tactics, and the MG 42 was a superb platform for this.

This soldier's Stahlhelm 42 has bread-bag straps attached, with foliage placed on it to aid concealment. He wears the 'M43' *Feldbluse*, which maintained most of the internal structure of the M36 and M41 variants, but the pocket pleats were completely eliminated, and the pockets were squared off. From 1943 onwards the lining and interior wound dressing pocket were mostly composed of rayon, and the number of buttons was reduced as a measure of economy and to speed production. By the end of 1943, the smartly pleated M36 and M41 *Feldblusen* were largely supplanted, although veterans still wore them, and some continued to be issued on occasion. The use of all sorts of material, including rayon and various forms of cellulose, served to reduce the quality, and to some extent the appearance, of the *Feldbluse*.

(3) *Kanonier*, Panzer-Artillerie-Regiment GD

This burly artilleryman is picking up a 10.5cm shell. Both 10.5cm and 15cm howitzers were added to IR (mot.) GD's firepower in the first half of 1941 as the unit started to resemble a miniature division more than a regiment. These weapons gave extremely capable support and were brutally effective against enemy infantry in the open, while also proving valuable against entrenched infantry and some armoured vehicles.

This soldier's single-decal Stahlhelm 35 has the chinstrap looped over the front brim. He has removed his *Feldbluse* and personal gear and wears the standard Heer service shirt with GD red-piped *Schulterklappen* attached, as well as the standard M43 trousers and ankle-boots.

(4) *Schulterstücke*, *Leutnant*, Panzergrenadier-Division GD

Officers wore metallic 'GD' ciphers that pushed through the *Schulterstücke* (shoulder boards) with prongs that were folded on the underside of the *Schulterstück* to hold the cipher in place.

GD soldiers, some with foliage attached to their helmets, crew a 7.5cm PaK 40 anti-tank gun near Bryansk, August 1943. The gun's prime mover, an SdKfz 11 half-track, can be seen behind the PaK 40. (ullstein bild/ullstein bild via Getty Images)

OPPOSITE
This summer-weight five-button *Feldbluse* bears the rank insignia of an *Oberleutnant* of PzArtRgt GD. Awards displayed here include the *EK I*, the *EK II*, the *Verwundetenabzeichen 1939 in Schwarz* and the *Krimschild* (Crimea Shield), awarded to troops fighting under Generalfeldmarschall Erich von Manstein in the campaign to capture Crimea during 1941–42. (INTERFOTO/Alamy Stock Photo)

Zitadelle. Those that did recover ran into the massed web of Soviet defences that slowly eroded their strength and exploited their vulnerable side and rear armour.

For much of *Zitadelle*, the weather was also extremely uncooperative. Heavy intermittent rains pelted PzGrenDiv GD's troops throughout the operation (Spaeter 1995: 115). While this might seem like a minor hindrance, it is important to remember that the vast majority of the Soviet Union's roads were unimproved and quickly turned to mud. The wider area of operations also held creeks, small rivers and ravines that could rapidly overflow; and even those fields that had no mines could become muddy pits that threatened to bog tanks, and the swampy areas became even more impassable. Lastly, but of no less importance, the rain made rest for the division's troops in the open almost impossible. The strains of combat, combined with the lack of proper rest, had a devastating impact on the combat effectiveness of the division's troops.

During the course of the 12 days of *Zitadelle*, PzGrenDiv GD advanced in the general direction of Oboyan (Spaeter 1995: 117 & 131). For the first time in the division's experience, Soviet air power became a major factor. Soviet aircraft, especially the Il-2 *Sturmovik* ground-attack aircraft, were omnipresent during the offensive and attacked with increased regularity (Spaeter 1995: 125). The Soviet counter-attacks never ceased during *Zitadelle*; but unlike the ill-conceived and poorly led Soviet counter-attacks so common in 1941 and the first half of 1942, these were better led. In addition, the sheer depth of Soviet reserves prepared for the defensive battle seemed almost limitless.

Like other German units, PzGrenDiv GD found itself continually bleeding offensive strength, not only through battle losses, but because increasing numbers of troops had to be detached to maintain flank security. On 12 July, most German offensive operations were suspended due to the Allied invasion of Sicily; large-scale Soviet counter-offensives elsewhere in the Soviet Union exacerbated the crisis. Very shortly thereafter, German units began to be transferred to the West. PzGrenDiv GD endured extremely heavy defensive fighting during 15 and 16 July; *Zitadelle* would provide to be the division's high tide.

Personnel of Ersatz-Brigade GD undertake training on a quad 2cm FlaK 38 anti-aircraft gun, November 1943. The NCO at left appears to be wearing riding breeches with ankle-boots and gaiters. In common with 3.7cm anti-aircraft weapons, the 2cm autocannons were highly effective against ground targets such as light armoured vehicles, fortifications and buildings. (Scherl/Süddeutsche Zeitung Photo/Alamy Stock Photo)

The remainder of 1943 consisted of a series of protracted withdrawals and often improvised defensive actions for PzGrenDiv GD and for the Wehrmacht as a whole in the East. For the main body of the division, there would be no major offensive operations after *Zitadelle*. By the end of 1943, many of the best German units on the Eastern Front were being transferred to rest and refit in North-West Europe in preparation for the anticipated Allied invasion of France.

A two-man *Pionier* team in training with a Flammenwerfer 41, Berlin, November 1943. The FmW 41 flamethrower had two different wands: one had a conventional pilot light arrangement at the end, while the other contained a blank-firing gun that used an especially hot 9×19mm blank, allowing the operator to spray the target with a stream of fuel oil by pulling the activating lever on the top of the wand part of the way back, then light the stream thereafter by pulling the level the rest of the way back activating the blank and igniting the stream of fuel oil and the previously sprayed fuel oil that now saturated the target. (Süddeutsche Zeitung Photo/Alamy Stock Photo)

From mid-1943, the Soviet forces facing the men of PzGrenDiv GD were much better trained, equipped and led than their predecessors. The near-continuous setbacks and defensive posture experienced by Axis forces began to take a toll on divisional morale, with a combination of exhaustion, losses and retreat creating a perfect storm (Showalter 2013: 271). This was not confined to GD. Across most of the Eastern Front, the Red Army's 'pressure everywhere' policy met Hitler's 'defend everything' policy and the Wehrmacht lost the competition.

Walter Hörnlein's medals, *Ärmelstreifen* and *Schulterstücke* are displayed with a commemorative box presented to him when he handed command of PzGrenDiv GD to Generalleutnant Hasso von Manteuffel in the first weeks of 1944. His awards include the 1914 EK I ribbon with 1939 *Spange*, the Sudetenland Medal, a World War I *Verwundetenabzeichen in Schwarz* and two different long-service medals, the circular one for four years and the cross for 18 years. The shoulderboard bearing the number '69' dates from his time as a battalion commander in Infanterie-Regiment 69 during 1935–37. (INTERFOTO/Alamy Stock Photo)

OPERATIONS IN 1944

The situation stabilized for PzGrenDiv GD by the beginning of 1944, as both sides were exhausted and needed time to regroup. Like the vast majority of the German forces at this stage in the conflict, the division was now fighting a series of defensive battles and would do so until the end of the war.

In early January, the division was involved in fighting around Kirovograd (now Kropyvnytskyi in Ukraine), striving to blunt and then repel the attacking forces of the Soviet 5th Guards Tank Army (Spaeter 1995: 273). Operating under command of the 8. Armee, the division was successful in this effort, allowing neighbouring German units to consolidate their positions and improve their defences. On 16 January, the division was bolstered by the Panthers of I./PzRgt 26, notionally part of the 26. Panzer-Division serving in Italy, but destined to fight under the command of PzGrenDiv GD on the Eastern Front. Having led PzGrenDiv GD through many months of savage combat, Generalleutnant Hörnlein relinquished command of the division in late January. A lull in the fighting in February allowed the division to reorganize

Oberst Karl Lorenz (in *Schirmmütze*) with Oberleutnant Hans Wentzke (in *Einheitsfeldmütze* and *Splittertarn* smock) and other GD personnel, Romania, January 1944. The man at left with the ammunition box wears a *Zeltbahn* shelter-quarter, while the rifleman at right wears a reversible cold-weather garment. (Bundesarchiv, Bild 101I-711-0428-28A/Theodor Scheerer /CC-BY-SA 3.0 de)

War volunteers with newly issued kit conveyed in their *Zeltbahnen* follow an *Unteroffizier* of PzRgt GD, 26 January 1944. The NCO wears a pullover under his *Panzerjacke*, and the trousers issued to armoured troops; these were somewhat loose and featured slant front pockets and two rear pockets that buttoned, in addition to a watch pocket on the front right of the trousers. They were bloused either with the tall jackboot or the low boots, but the low boots are much more prominent in period photos from 1943 onwards. (Süddeutsche Zeitung Photo/ Alamy Stock Photo)

and regroup before the Soviet offensive resumed in earnest on 8 March (Spaeter 1995: 288). Oberst Otto Büsing, the commander of PzRgt GD, died of wounds sustained during the notably severe Soviet bombardment of

Troops of PzFüsRgt GD in action, 10 March 1944. Throughout the life of PzGrenDiv GD, there appears to have been a strong rivalry between the veterans of PzGrenRgt GD and the less-experienced troops of PzFüsRgt GD. (Scherl/Süddeutsche Zeitung Photo/Alamy Stock Photo)

Horst Niemack and other GD personnel attend Hitlerjugend training, 11 March 1944. (Heinrich Hoffmann/ullstein bild via Getty Images)

PzGrenDiv GD's positions on that day, along with several other respected officers and soldiers of the division. Under intolerable pressure, the various units subordinated to PzGrenDiv GD conducted a fighting withdrawal as the deep cold of the early weeks of 1944 gave way to seemingly bottomless mud.

Now led by Generalleutnant Hasso von Manteuffel, its most famous commander, the division was still operating under the command of the 8. Armee in April, seeking to defend Germany's ally Romania from the threat of Soviet invasion (Glantz 2007: 65–69). Manteuffel's division was involved in especially fierce fighting around the Romanian town of Târgu Frumos (Buttar 2020: 346–49). Captured by Soviet forces on 9 April, Târgu Frumos was swiftly recaptured by PzGrenDiv GD on 9–10 April, with 40 Panthers and 40 Tigers mounting an attack from the east of the town in concert with Romanian infantry. Following this success, Manteuffel deployed PzGrenRgt GD north-west of the town and PzFüsRgt GD north-east and east, with PzRgt GD held in readiness behind the centre of the German position. PzGrenDiv GD was assigned to hold this area and prevent the Soviets from penetrating into the Romanian interior. The defensive effort was consolidated by skilful reconnaissance, with Unteroffizier Johannes Evangelist 'Hans' Röger of 1./PzFüsRgt GD awarded the *Ritterkreuz* for infiltrating the Soviet lines wearing civilian clothing. Hauptmann Bernhard Klemz, the commander of 5./PzRgt GD, also received the *Ritterkreuz*, in recognition of his PzKpfw IV-equipped company's efforts to capture an important ridge near the town on 25 April, and to engage and destroy a Soviet armour unit as they assembled

Generalleutnant Hasso von Manteuffel, the commander of PzGrenDiv GD, is pictured with (left) Oberst Horst Niemack, commander of PzFüsRgt GD, and (right) Oberst Wilhelm Langkeit, commander of PzRgt GD, in 1944. After serving as a cavalry officer in World War I, Manteuffel served as a Panzer commander in the Soviet Union, winning the *RK* in December 1941, before leading a division in Tunisia in 1942–43. Promoted to *Generalmajor* on 1 May 1943, he commanded the 7. Panzer-Division on the Eastern Front until being appointed the commander of PzGrenDiv GD on 1 February 1944. He led GD until he was given command of the 5. Panzerarmee as a *General der Panzertruppe* on 1 September 1944, subsequently leading his army with distinction during the Battle of the Bulge (16 December 1944–25 January 1945). Horst Niemack won the *RK* in July 1940 and the *Eichenlaub* in August 1941 following an encirclement operation in which he was seriously wounded. After winning the *Schwerten* (Swords) and being wounded again in August 1944, Niemack recovered to lead the Panzer-Lehr-Division until war's end. Wilhelm 'Willy' Langkeit fought in Poland, France and the Soviet Union with a variety of anti-tank and armoured units, being evacuated from Stalingrad in 1943. Promoted to *Oberst* on 1 December 1943, he was given command of PzRgt GD on 1 March 1944 and led the unit until he was severely wounded on 15 October 1944, subsequently commanding Panzergrenadier-Division 'Kurmark' until war's end. (ullstein bild/ullstein bild via Getty Images)

A *Panzerschreck* team load their weapon as they take cover in a ruined building, 1944. See also p.57. (Scherl/Süddeutsche Zeitung Photo/Alamy Stock Photo)

during the night of 26/27 April. The fighting was the first occasion on which the division encountered the IS-2, the Red Army's newly fielded heavy tank with a 122mm main gun. Oberleutnant Diddo Diddens, the commander of 1./StuGAbt GD, received the *Eichenlaub* for his part in the 25 April battle.

As the fighting around Târgu Frumos intensified in early May, the Soviet massed attacks threatened to be overwhelming with substantial numbers of tanks and infantry thrown at PzGrenDiv GD's positions in wave after wave (Glantz 2007: 215). Nevertheless, the division's defences held. According to Soviet sources, the division's troops were solidly entrenched in bunkers with excellent cover and proved able to deal considerable losses to the attackers

GD troops aboard a StuG IV fitted with *Schürzen* (side armour) near Jassy (modern-day Iaşi), Romania, April–May 1944. By this date the *Einheitsfeldmütze* ('universal' cap) is in evidence – although the crewman with headphones retains the older *Feldmütze* – and two MG 42 machine guns, one with bipod and drum magazine fitted, can be seen. (ullstein bild/ullstein bild via Getty Images)

(Glantz 2007: 219). Well equipped with automatic weapons including the StG 44 assault rifle, Manteuffel's troops utilized well-placed artillery support and local counter-attacks to savage the Soviet advances once they had been identified, helping to restore the Axis line on numerous occasions during the battle (Buttar 2020: 339). The division's armour, particularly the Tigers and Panthers, were especially aggressive, turning many local actions into serious Soviet defeats and enabling the division to get the better of much more numerous adversaries.

Jassy, April 1944: these Tiger I heavy tanks have Zimmerit, a paste-like coating intended to protect the tank from magnetic mines, applied to their hull surfaces. The Tiger leaving the road also has track-links supplementing the frontal armour. Although it sported flat-sided, vertical armour, the Tiger remained almost invulnerable to most Allied tank and anti-tank guns throughout the war in the frontal arc. Equipped with the formidable 8.8cm KwK 36 L/56 gun, the Tiger was heavier and slower than the Panther; it was especially vulnerable to swamping in soft ground. Expensive to produce, the Tiger was so large it had to be fitted with a totally separate set of tracks to be transported by train. It was just as vulnerable to attack from the side as any other tank, and it was difficult to recover due to its size. Although PzGrenDiv GD's workshops often worked around the clock in breakneck shifts to repair battle-damaged tanks and vehicles, if the Tiger required major refitting or repair, it had to be returned to Germany. (ullstein bild/ullstein bild via Getty Images)

From 11 May, the Târgu Frumos sector became quiet and Manteuffel took the opportunity to rest, refit and reorganize the troops under his command. Oberst Fritz von Bandelow's Grenadier-Regiment 1029, a scratch force formed from GD personnel in March 1944 to bolster the Hungarian and Romanian regimes in the face of possible *coup d'état* attempts, was disbanded and its personnel were absorbed by PzGrenDiv GD; PzArtRgt GD re-formed its IV. Abteilung; I./PzFüsRgt GD was sent back to Germany to refit and train as an armoured infantry battalion; and PzAufklAbt GD received the new Hetzer tank destroyer and half-tracked armoured personnel carriers (Spaeter 1995: 337).

PzGrenDiv GD was involved in heavy fighting around Jassy in early June, with Major Helmut Süssman, the commander of II./PzArtRgt GD, being killed on 3 June. The division was eventually withdrawn in mid-June; despite its defensive successes, events elsewhere conspired to degrade the German war effort permanently (Schaulen 1983: 133). The summer of 1944 witnessed both the Allied invasion of France during Operation *Overlord* (6 June) and the destruction of Heeresgruppe Mitte during Operation *Bagration* (22 June–19 August).

In late July the division prepared for a move north, into East Prussia, then moved into combat on 5 August around Vilkaviškis, Lithuania. Several days of combat on the German/Lithuanian border ensued, with Vilkaviškis briefly falling to the division only to be recaptured by the Red Army on 18 August. The division was relieved and participated in efforts to re-establish contact with elements of Heeresgruppe Nord besieged in Riga, then adopted a defensive posture near Kuršėnai. On 1 September Manteuffel handed command of the division to Oberst Lorenz and took command of the 5. Panzerarmee in the West. Promoted to *Generalmajor* in November 1944, Lorenz would lead the division through the final months of the war.

A GD Panzer *Oberleutnant* brandishes a *Leuchtpistole* (flare pistol), used for signalling, May 1944. He wears the *Panzerjacke* over a pullover and paler legwear, and retains the *Feldmütze*, in this case in black. His awards include the *EK I*, the *Panzerkampfabzeichen* and the *Verwundetenabzeichen in Silber*. (ullstein bild/ullstein bild via Getty Images)

GD troops near Jassy, 1944. Note the continued presence of the MG 34, the addition of Heer breast eagle and *Schulterklappen* to one man's shirt, and the fact that neither man has his helmet chinstrap in use. (Keystone-France/Gamma-Keystone via Getty Images)

In October, PzGrenDiv GD was involved in the confused fighting in the Memel bridgehead. Meanwhile, the tankers of I./PzRgt GD, deployed separately from the rest of PzRgt GD, were in combat under command of the 6. Panzer-Division near Różan on the Narew River; Unteroffizier Rudolf Larsen, a Panther commander, won the *Ritterkreuz* for his actions during 4–9 October 1944. After more than a year, Larsen's battalion finally rejoined PzGrenRgt GD in mid-November, allowing I./PzRgt 26 to be withdrawn and redeployed.

As PzGrenDiv GD continued to fight on the Eastern Front, elements associated with the division played a major role behind the front lines. During the first half of 1944, the FBB continued to guard key command centres while preparing for front-line combat. Expanded first to regimental and then to

Wary GD troops including an MG 42 machine-gun team watch the skies, August 1944. Note the machine-gunner's ammunition pouch worn by the man in the foreground, and the continued use of the *Feldmütze* by the NCO at left. The SdKfz 251 in the background is camouflaged with foliage that reveals the *Balkenkreuz* on the vehicle's side. (Süddeutsche Zeitung Photo/Alamy Stock Photo)

The Gew 43 rifle began to be issued to GD personnel in early 1944. It was a gas-operated, piston-driven rifle that fired the full-sized 7.92×57mm cartridge fed from a ten-round box magazine. In general, the Gew 43 was well-received. It was capable of quite good accuracy, and the rapid follow-up shots made it popular. Most of the rifles were fitted with a siderail mount that allowed the user to fit a ZF4 optical sight to the rifle. (Armémuseum (The Swedish Army Museum)/Wikimedia/CC BY-SA 4.0)

brigade status, the unit played a key role in two important events that shaped the course of the war: the aftermath of the attempted assassination of Hitler on 20 July; and the Battle of the Bulge (16 December 1944–25 January 1945).

G IN RETREAT, 1944

(1) Panzerfüsilier

This private soldier of PzFüsRgt GD is armed with the StG 44 assault rifle, Initially designated the Maschinenpistole 43 (MP 43) and then Maschinenpistole 44 (MP 44), it was a operated, piston-driven, select-fire rifle fed by a 30-round detachable box magazine. The selector was a bar that slid from left to right to switch from full-auto to semi-auto fire. By 1943, the basic and refined MP 43 and MP 43/1 were issued in limited numbers in the East, and PzGrenDiv GD may have received a few of these. They were very popular with the troops for obvious reasons. Variants and experiments with the series of rifles presaged developments far ahead of the StG 44's time. While the entire series had threaded muzzles with screw-on muzzle protectors, some also had siderails that were intended to fit a specially designed scope mount that accommodated the ZF4 optical sight. Towards the end of World War II, the first standard-issue night sight, the Vampir, was also produced in extremely limited quantities for the StG 44; it is unclear whether these ever made their way to PzGrenDiv GD.

This soldier's equipment includes the enlisted man's belt with StG 44 magazine pouches, bread bag with canteen and mess kit mounted, webbing Y-straps and gasmask canister. The StG 44 utilized a 7.92mm bullet, but seated in a shorter cartridge case and with an overall length of only 33mm. This allowed the user to carry far more ammunition for a similar weight. Whereas the standard 7.92×57mm round weighed 197 grains, the 7.92×33mm round weighed 123 grains, with powder and case weights being greatly reduced as well. Virtually all of the issued 7.92×33mm ammunition was steel-cased, and tracers and blanks were available. Each StG 44-armed soldier was ideally issued with six or seven magazines, to be carried in two three-cell magazine pouches on the front of the belt. The availability of magazines and pouches never kept up with demand, however, and soldiers are often shown wearing only one pouch and carrying only three or four magazines. The construction of the pouches varies widely; there appears to have been no standard, but rather a number of different designs. The most commonly represented are the 'feed bag' magazine pouches. These and other pouches were in theory supposed to have a strap that ran around the back to help support the weight of the magazines and ammunition.

He wears the splinter-pattern padded parka and helmet cover, toque, M43 trousers and ankle-boots with gaiters.

(2) Unteroffizier, Panzer-Pionier-Bataillon GD

Armed with an MP 40 submachine gun, this NCO wears the M41 Feldbluse with M43 trousers and jackboots. His decorations include the EK II and Ostmedaille ribbons in the second buttonhole, with the EK I, Allgemeines Sturmabzeichen (General Assault Badge) and Verwundetenabzeichen in Silber on the left breast pocket.

(3) Schütze, Führer-Begleit-Bataillon

This Panzerschreck-armed soldier wears the M43 Einheitsfeldmütze with the reversible parka and trousers with the white side out; his whitewashed Stahlhelm 42 hangs from his enlisted man's waist belt. Padded jackets and trousers began to be issued towards the beginning of winter in late 1943. The initial production run of these was in a shade known as Mausgrau (mouse grey). The outside covering was a medium–heavy cotton or rayon material in the early batches. Some padded jackets and trousers were reversible to white, and many of the GD troops found this 'instant' snow camouflage particularly useful. Most of the jackets also had an attached hood that helped keep the biting wind at bay.

The interior of these jackets and trousers was generally composed of layers of blanket-like material. The cuffs and neck could be fitted snugly to retain heat in cold conditions. The initial batches of these winter garments do not appear to have been camouflaged, other than the reversible white. One slightly unforeseen effect of the large-scale issue of this snow camouflage was 'blue-on-blue' incidents; German troops in white looked just like Soviet troops in white. The simple solution arrived at by some GD personnel and eventually issued was a coloured armband to identify friend from foe. Surviving issued armbands are generally reversible from blue to red.

GD soldiers, one with rolled-up sleeves and carrying an MG 34, move forward alongside a Panther medium tank in July 1944, by which time many of the type's initial faults had been rectified. Utilizing the T-34's sloped-armour concept, the Panther could achieve speeds up to about 55km/h, but was susceptible to muddy and boggy ground – a significant handicap for PzGrenDiv GD's Panthers at Kursk. The gearbox was plagued with issues, a problem that seems to have been recognized beforehand, but not rectified before Kursk. At ranges of less than 1,000m, the 7.5cm KwK 42 L/70 main gun was lethal to any Allied tank of 1943 from any angle. The gun also fired a very effective high-explosive shell, and the Wehrmacht's well-trained gunners and the Panther's excellent optics combined to give the gun/tank combination a fearsome reputation. (ullstein bild/ullstein bild via Getty Images)

In the hours after the assassination attempt, the FBB was led by Major Otto Ernst Remer, a GD veteran and an avowed supporter of Hitler's regime who acted swiftly to restore order following the bombing (Caddick-Adams 2015: 228–29). At first Remer followed the orders given to him by chief conspirator Oberst Claus von Stauffenberg, which specified that he should arrest senior members of the Nazi leadership as they were seeking to overthrow the regime. When Remer arrived at the office of Joseph Goebbels, however, the Propaganda Minister convinced him that Hitler was still alive and that he should crush Stauffenberg and his associates in Berlin. Operating alongside SS units, Remer quickly used the men under his command to bring Berlin under control for the regime, an effort praised by the Nazi leadership; this is likely what kept the division in Hitler's good graces for the remaining months of the war.

Lionized by the regime, Remer would return to front-line soldiering, with limited success. Expanded to brigade status, Remer's unit participated in the Battle of the Bulge, notably during the fighting for St. Vith, a struggle that came to exemplify the dogged defence by US forces in the Ardennes against well-trained and -led German veterans (Merriam 2012: 57). St. Vith was the hub of a vital road network, much like the more famous Bastogne, and although the battle received less attention, the actions there were important. The failure of the German forces to take St. Vith in a timely manner resulted in massive disruption to an already fragile offensive. St. Vith became a vital 'speed bump' for US forces. According to Remer's own report written after the war, the stubborn resistance mounted by the mixed group of Americans defending the city forced the FBB north of St. Vith on to an already clogged road network, with cross-country movement being almost impossible (Remer 1947: 8–9).

The FBB was redirected multiple times during the course of the battle, often apparently at Hitler's personal whim, and participated in the fighting

Otto Ernst Remer, photographed in 1944, wears the *Ritterkreuz mit Eichenlaub*, awarded on 12 November 1943, as well as the *Deutsches Kreuz in Gold* and a Bulgarian award on his right breast and the *EK I* and a pair of wound badges on his left breast. After extensive combat service on the Eastern Front and subsequent appointment to lead the Wachbataillon GD, Remer played a major role in stopping the 20 July plot to assassinate Hitler. In 1944–45 he commanded the Führer-Begleit-Brigade, notably in the Ardennes, before being captured by the US Army. Imprisoned until 1947, Remer was active in far-right politics in West Germany before fleeing to Egypt. Returning to West Germany in the 1980s, he once again faced criminal charges arising from his political activities and fled to Spain, where he died on 4 October 1997. (ullstein bild/ullstein bild via Getty Images)

A GD NCO wearing the *RK* instructs a Hitlerjugend member in the use of the disposable, single-shot *Panzerfaust* or 'Tank Fist', November 1944. The first *Panzerfaust* – the 30 or 'klein' (small model), sometimes referred to as 'Gretchen' – had a range of 30m and was effective against any Allied tank encountered at the time. As the size of the *Panzerfaust* increased as the war progressed (60, 100), the size of the warhead and the range also increased, giving GD's men enhanced tank-killing capacity at ever-greater distances. (Süddeutsche Zeitung Photo/Alamy Stock Photo)

OPPOSITE

Members of PzGrenDiv GD make loopholes in an East Prussian house, November 1944. Both men wear the *Einheitsfeldmütze*. (Scherl/Süddeutsche Zeitung Photo/Alamy Stock Photo)

at Bastogne as well. Diverted away from Bastogne to try to disentangle other German units beginning to experience significant trouble, the FBB was redirected again towards Bastogne just as the entire German offensive was beginning to lose momentum, and the long arduous retreat began for German forces. During the course of the Battle of the Bulge, three members of the FBB were awarded the *Ritterkreuz*: Oberwachtmeister Max Holm of 1./PzRgt FBB; Rittmeister Leonhard von Möllendorf, the commander of III./FBB, who was mortally wounded leading a counter-attack; and Feldwebel Kurt Scheunemann of 2./PzRgt FBB.

Another unit that would achieve prominence in the latter part of 1944, the Führer-Grenadier-Brigade (FGB) assembled at Fallingbostel in late August, entering combat near Gumbinnen (modern-day Gusev, Russia) during the last week of October. Under the command of the 4. Armee, the FGB acquitted itself well, facilitating the German recapture of Goldap (modern-day Gołdap, Poland), the first German city to fall to Soviet forces. In December the FGB left the Eastern Front and headed west, destined for the Ardennes offensive.

By December 1944, after another series of arduous retreats following the collapse of the front in the summer, PzGrenDiv GD was re-formed as a fully-fledged *Panzerkorps*, which it would remain until the end of the war. General der Panzertruppe Dietrich von Saucken would lead the new corps until February, being succeeded by General der Panzertruppe Georg Jauer. The various units of the elite PzGrenDiv 'Brandenburg' were also brought under Panzerkorps GD's umbrella, and the corps remained one of the most powerful and well-equipped German formations until the end of the war.

Reichsminister for Propaganda Josef Goebbels receives a GD *Ärmelstreifen* from Generalmajor Karl Lorenz, the divisional commander. Lorenz wears the standard general officer's *Schirmmütze* and *Mantel* with the GD officer's *Ärmelstreifen*. He saw action with the *Pionier* branch in Poland, France and the Soviet Union before joining GD as the commander of PzPiBtl GD in August 1942, subsequently being given command of PzGrenRgt GD as a *Major* after Otto Köhler's death on 1 December that year. Promoted to *Oberstleutnant* in February 1943 and *Oberst* in August 1943, he succeeded Hasso von Manteuffel as divisional commander on 1 September 1944 and led GD until war's end. (Heinrich Hoffmann/ullstein bild via Getty Images)

A GD NCO trains Volkssturm ('People's Militia') personnel, East Prussia, November 1944. (ullstein bild/ullstein bild via Getty Images)

OPERATIONS IN 1945

The various elements of Panzerkorps GD were widely dispersed throughout Germany and its remaining allied and occupied territories during January–May 1945. With the Allied forces closing in on both sides, various schools, depots and other sub-units of all branches of the German armed forces were rapidly thrown into action in *Kampfgruppen* (battlegroups) throughout the Reich.

The bulk of GD's forces were deployed in the East, but somewhat scattered. In late January, StuGBrig GD and PzPiBtl GD became involved in a major action around the Polish city of Łódź and its environs. The jumbled railway arrangements meant that equipment went missing, never to be retrieved, but that did not stop the *Sturmgeschütze* and *Pioniere* from mounting a stubborn defence that allowed neighbouring German units to execute controlled withdrawals westwards in the face of heavy Soviet attacks, following detraining. The Soviet advances were almost too fast for the trains, and at times, GD's assault guns withdrew with Soviet tanks on parallel roads advancing almost as quickly (Spaeter 2000: 183–85).

GD personnel continued to be awarded numerous decorations. On 24 February Hauptmann Horst Warschnauer, the commander of PzPiBtl GD, was awarded the *Eichenlaub* in recognition of his conduct during the heavy fighting in East Prussia. PzPiBtl GD recaptured the town of Maulen from Soviet forces before assaulting a key hilltop position, during which Warschnauer rallied his men after the attack stalled and successfully stormed the hill, enabling other German forces to withdraw safely. Warschnauer would die in British captivity on 26 December 1948, two days before his 29th birthday.

GD personnel show a *Panzerschreck* to a group of boys. Two of the GD men, including the NCO, have a blanket roll over the left shoulder in the Soviet style. The NCO's Heer breast eagle appears to be on dark bluish-green badge cloth, as are his *Schulterklappen*, while his *Feldmütze* lacks the *Soutache* in branch-of-service colour. The Panzerraketenbüsche 43 or *Panzerschreck* ('Tank Terror'), a German copy of the American bazooka, operated on basically identical principles with a small electrical generator initiating firing of a hollow-charge warhead. This created a jet stream that bored its way through steel armour, sending molten shrapnel throughout the interior of the vehicle, destroying crew and equipment and often setting off on-board ammunition, resulting in catastrophic kills. The *Panzerschreck* utilized an 8.8cm rocket that could penetrate about 100mm of armour plate. It was effective within about 90m and was usually crewed by a gunner and a loader. The *Panzerschreck* was sometimes fitted with a shield to protect the gunner from back blast, but these also seem to have been removed due to the fact that they made the weapon significantly bulkier to wield. The *Panzerschreck* was very simple to learn to use, but its significant blast gave away the firing position to the alert. (Süddeutsche Zeitung Photo/Alamy Stock Photo)

General der Panzertruppe Dietrich von Saucken, the commander of Panzerkorps GD during the winter of 1944/45. A World War I veteran, Saucken fought in Poland, France, the Balkans and the Soviet Union, leading the 4. Panzer-Division during the battle of Kursk and assuming command of III. Panzerkorps in May 1944. After being relieved of command of Panzerkorps GD after a dispute about the futility of continuing the war, Saucken was appointed commander of the 2. Armee until war's end. Saucken wears the *Ritterkreuz mit Eichenlaub und Schwertern*; on 9 May 1945, he was the last German soldier to receive the *Brillanten* (Diamonds), a distinction he shared with Hermann Balck and Hasso von Manteuffel. (Heinrich Hoffmann/ullstein bild via Getty Images)

OPPOSITE

This *Panzerjacke* bears the insignia of a *Feldwebel* of StuGAbt GD, including an *EK II* ribbon, a signaller qualification badge on the left sleeve and a *Panzervernichtungsabzeichen* (Tank Destruction Badge) *in Silber* on the right sleeve. Panzer crews wore black uniforms while StuG crews wore field-grey uniforms. Although an exterior pocket was added to lightweight herringbone twill jackets issued in small quantities later in the war, the standard wool jacket had no protruding exterior pockets. Again, this was to facilitate movement inside the vehicle. The jackets featured button cuffs on the sleeves that allowed for some ventilation. In addition, the jacket contained not one but two wound dressing pockets. One pocket usually held a conventional wound dressing, and the other held a special dressing designed to treat burns. Note the dark bluish-green cloth used for the *Schulterklappen* and the backing for the Heer breast eagle. (INTERFOTO/ Alamy Stock Photo)

One of the smaller ad hoc units created from some of GD's components was Alarmverband 'Schmelter', formed from part of a *Panzerjäger* unit belonging to GD, but not under GD's direct command. This was typical of the haphazard creation and deployment of German units that was very common in the closing weeks of the war. The unit was formed for the local defence of Cottbus, but it was moved seemingly randomly from point to point with no very clear objective, encountering scattered action along the way that depleted the unit in men and *matériel* for no real gain

(Spaeter 2000: 191–93). These units were lucky to receive Heer or Waffen-SS cadres and recruits at this point, as increasingly Volkssturm (People's Militia) and even Kriegsmarine (Navy) units were being used to create the very mixed groups of theoretical fighting formations. GD was steadily depleted in scattered fighting across the shrinking Reich.

H THE FINAL MONTHS, 1945

(1) *Oberfüsilier*, **Panzer-Füsilier-Regiment GD**

Clad in a *Sumpftarn*-camouflage smock, this sniper is armed with a Kar 98k 'High Turret' sniping rifle. Amid the wartime simplifications and substitutions, the amount and types of camouflage clothing was actually expanded. During 1944, GD's men began to receive new camouflage smocks and helmet covers made of the newer *Sumpftarn*, commonly referred to as 'Tan and Water' by collectors and modern-day scholars. This camouflage pattern had much softer, blended and blurred edges than the *Splittertarn* material. As with earlier smocks and helmet covers, some but not all were reversible. Construction was similar to earlier smocks, but some of the newer smocks had an integral face net that obscured the wearer's visage under combat conditions. The padded winter clothing was also issued in this new pattern, and again, some items were reversible. The construction changed little, but wartime shortages led to substitutions for the insulating material inside the jacket. One final camouflage pattern, *Leibermuster*, was issued on a limited basis in 1945, but none of it is recorded as being issued to GD, and no known photographic evidence supports its use by GD personnel.

His webbing Y-straps support the standard enlisted man's waist belt with rifle magazine pouches. Although designed for tropical use, web equipment belts and Y-straps became more commonplace general issue in 1944, regardless of the environment. Beginning in 1944, the bread bag had a pocket added to the exterior, but under the flap, for the rifle-cleaning kit. The rings on the back for the bread-bag strap were sometimes omitted. In addition, the loops on bread bags produced from 1944 were often webbing rather than leather. Metal cups on canteens became less common, and some truly odd colours of Bakelite cup such as orange and a sort of seafoam green became more common. Canteen bodies were more frequently made of painted or enamelled steel, and mess kits also became more commonly made out of enamelled steel. Very small numbers of the last model of Seitengewehr 84/98 III bayonet were also issued that had what amounted to a period 'multi-tool' built into the grip.

Late in 1944, plastic equipment belts began to appear, as well as plastic bayonet frogs and Kar 98k magazine pouches. Other equipment is rumoured to have been made in this material, but it is very hard to discern in period photographs, which become far scarcer in late 1944 and 1945.

(2) *Leutnant*, **Panzer-Pionier-Bataillon GD**

This junior officer wears the last model of *Feldbluse* issued to GD, the 'M44'; this was a vast departure from earlier designs. The portion below the waist and the bottom pockets were completely eliminated to conserve material. This obviously eliminated the belt suspension system, but the wound dressing pocket was retained in many and merely moved a bit higher. Some M44 *Feldblusen* were made with 'Italian wool', a rather fine grade of uniform wool from appropriated Italian

stocks, while others, usually those in the brownish tones, were made with notably lower-grade materials and inferior dyes.

The last pattern of issue trousers, usually referred to as *Kielhosen*, began to be issued in 1944. These had less material at the waist and an integral belt, at least in many cases; they were designed specifically to be worn with low boots, and were made of a number of different materials. These generally fitted well with the M44 *Feldbluse*.

(3) *Panzergrenadier*, **Panzergrenadier-Regiment GD**

Armed with the StG 44 assault rifle, this private soldier is unscrewing the cap on a 3kg hollow-charge magnetic anti-tank mine. GD's infantry and *Pioniere* used two basic types of mines: anti-personnel and anti-tank. Anti-personnel mines were smaller, held less explosive, and were detonated by tripwires or relatively small amounts of pressure, whereas anti-tank mines could require many kilogrammes of pressure to detonate.

The most dreaded of all German anti-personnel mines was the Springmine 35, aka the S-Mine, essentially one small cylindrical metal case set inside another. At the bottom of the exterior case sat a small charge. When the mine was triggered, this charge shot the interior case to a height of about 1m, where the mine detonated. The inside of the mine was filled with ball bearings. The mine could be detonated by stepping on the fuze then letting off the pressure (when the victim lifted a foot) or via a tripwire. The S-Mine was simplified slightly in 1944, and the ball bearings were replaced with langrage, basically any sort of scrap ordnance materials that could be stuffed into the case. Appearing in 1942, the largely wooden Schützenmine 42, aka the *Schu-mine*, was extremely difficult to detect and had just enough of an explosive charge to debilitate a soldier, but usually not enough to kill. The Glasmine 43, with a glass body, was another difficult-to-detect mine that produced similar results.

The primary anti-tank mine available to GD's men early in the war was the Tellermine 35. These mines generally required a considerable amount of pressure to detonate, usually needing at least an armoured vehicle such as a light tank to pass over them. The Tellermine 35 could also be detonated by a fuze. This enabled the soldier to throw or pull the mine with a cord underneath the approaching tank or up onto its engine deck. In addition, GD's troops were also trained to approach the enemy tank from the side and throw the mine onto the tank's tracks as it passed. The mine then rode the tracks until it fell over the front, with the tank then running over the mine.

In 1944, the 3kg magnetic hollow-charge anti-tank mine, shown here, also began to appear. The funnel-shaped body was made of either wood or metal, with three magnets that locked onto a tank or other enemy vehicle. The user had to attach the mine to the enemy vehicle by hand. Just before attaching, he pulled a cord that ignited the fuze. The hollow charge was capable of knocking our virtually any Allied tank.

(4) **Fourth-type GD *Ärmelstreifen***

4 Großdeutschland

GD personnel amid the wreckage of retreat prepare to be evacuated from Balga, Germany (now in Kaliningrad Oblast, Russia), in early March 1945. (Albert Otto/ullsteinbild via Getty Images)

The Führer-Begleit-Brigade was redesignated the Führer-Begleit-Division (FBD) on 26 January 1945, but it never approached genuine divisional strength. Its commander, Otto Ernst Remer, a favourite of Hitler's, was promoted to *Generalmajor* and now commanded scraps of the FBD along with other units. Fighting as a *Kampfgruppe*, the remnants of Remer's division were wiped out or captured during the final weeks of fighting (Spaeter 2000: 428). Many of the division's most effective leaders – among them highly decorated veterans of multiple battles, such as *Ritterkreuz*-holder Oberleutnant Wilhelm Geisberg – died trying to preserve both manpower and fighting cohesion (Spaeter 2000: 429). While some personnel made their way home, most ended up buried anonymously in a field, or in British or American captivity if lucky, a Soviet prison camp if not.

CONCLUSION

In the postwar environment, GD maintained a strong reputation and many of its officers such as Hasso von Manteuffel either pursued careers in the Bundeswehr or became successful authors or technical advisers. The GD tradition association continued to meet until after 2010, though the number of veterans continued to dwindle. Although GD had 'dirty hands' – as did many if not most other German units, especially those that fought in the East – it was a remarkably effective combat organization that instilled a strong sense of *esprit de corps* among its soldiers and officers until the end, and its reputation as an elite combat formation was hard-earned.

Some of the personal effects of a former *Obergefreiter* of PzAufklAbt GD, including a *Feldmütze* with *Soutache*. (INTERFOTO/Alamy Stock Photo)

SELECT BIBLIOGRAPHY

Buttar, Prit (2020). *The Reckoning: The Defeat of Army Group South, 1944*. Oxford: Osprey Publishing.

Caddick-Adams, Peter (2015). *Snow and Steel: The Battle of the Bulge, 1944–45*. Oxford: Oxford University Press.

Doughty, Robert A. (1990). *The Breaking Point: Sedan and the Fall of France, 1940*. Hamden, CT: Archon.

Friesser, Karl-Heinz (2005). *The Blitzkrieg Legend: The 1940 Campaign and the Fall of France*. Annapolis, MD: Naval Institute Press.

Glantz, David M. (2007). *Red Storm Over the Balkans*. Lawrence, KS: University Press of Kansas.

Glantz, David M. & House, Jonathan M. (1999). *The Battle of Kursk*. Lawrence, KS: University Press of Kansas.

Merriam, Ray., ed. (2012). *The Battle of St. Vith, Belgium, 17-23 December, 1944: An Example of Armor in the Defense*. Bennington, VT: Merriam.

Pritchett, Scott (2010). *Uniforms and Insignia of the Großdeutschland Division*. Three volumes. Atglen, PA: Schiffer.

Remer, Otto Ernst, trans. C.E. Weber (1947). 'The Fuhrer Begleit Brigade (The Brigade Under the Command of Remer) in the Ardennes Offensive (16 December 44 to 26 January 45).' MS# B592.

Schaulen, Joachim von (1983). *Hasso von Manteufuel: Panzerkampf in Zweiten Weltkrieg*. Berg am See: Kurt Vowinckel.

Showalter, Dennis E. (2013). *Armor and Blood: The Battle of Kursk, the Turning Point of World War II*. New York, NY: Random House.

Spaeter, Helmut, trans. David Johnson (1992). *The History of Panzerkorps Großdeutschland, Volume 1*. Winnipeg: J.J. Fedorowicz.

Spaeter, Helmut, trans. David Johnson (1995). *The History of Panzerkorps Großdeutschland, Volume 2*. Winnipeg: J.J. Fedorowicz.

Spaeter, Helmut, trans. David Johnson (2000). *The History of Panzerkorps Großdeutschland, Volume 3*. Winnipeg: J.J. Fedorowicz.

INDEX